D1521766

Gordon D. McLeod

ESSENTIALLY CANADIAN

The Life and Fiction of Alan Sullivan 1868-1947

Allan Sullivan wrote over forty works of popular fiction between 1890 and 1940; today it is difficult to find even one copy of many of these works. A well-known and widely read author in the first half of this century, Sullivan wrote thrillers, historical romance, children's stories, and novels set in the north (*The Great Divide*, *The Fur Masters*, *Cariboo Road*). Now there is no complete collection of his published works anywhere in the world.

In this literary biography of Alan Sullivan, the author interweaves Sullivan's life story and his literary career. Drawing on published and unpublished material as well as on information supplied by Sullivan's four children, McLeod traces the influence on Sullivan's writings of his early years in Sault Ste. Marie and in mining and construction camps, of society life in Toronto, of visits to the Arctic and Europe, and residence on an English country estate. Sullivan is seen as a man whose essential characteristics are those of Canada, and whose literary work is parallelled by the paintings of the Group of Seven artists. His literary works are discussed and evaluated in the light of Sullivan's own and other Canadian critical theories.

The bibliography provides a convenient listing of Sullivan's book-length publications. The volume will be of value to students of literature, but will also appeal to anyone interested in Canadian life and culture.

Gordon D. McLeod, Associate Professor of English at Lakehead University, Thunder Bay, Ontario, received the Ph.D. degree in Canadian fiction from the University of Manitoba. In addition to writing review articles on Canadian fiction, he is co-author of A Theatre Happening.

Gordon D. McLeod

ESSENTIALLY CANADIAN

The Life and Fiction of Alan Sullivan 1868-1947

Wilfrid Laurier University Press

813
S949m

Canadian Cataloguing in Publication Data

McLeod, Gordon Duncan.
  Essentially Canadian : the life and fiction of
Alan Sullivan 1868-1947

Bibliography: p.
Includes index.
ISBN 0-88920-112-9

1. Sullivan, Alan, 1868-1947.   2. Authors,
Canadian (English) — 20th century — Biography.*
I. Title.

PS8537.U44Z7   C813'.52   C82-094514-5
PR9199.3.S84Z7

Cover design: Polygon Design Limited

83 - 8023

Dedicated
to the four charming children
of Alan Sullivan:

Kathleen, Lady Liddell Hart
Natalie, Madame Francois Coulet
Matthew Barry Sullivan
Michael Sullivan

Contents

List of Illustrations

Bishop Edward Sullivan—about 1890

Alan Sullivan (on top of large pipe) with two friends—Sault Ste. Marie, Ontario—1895

Alan Sullivan—in front of mine in northern Ontario—late 1890s

Bessie Hees Sullivan—at the time of her wedding—1900

Alan Sullivan with his son D'Arcy—1910

Alan Sullivan—1925

Alan Sullivan—1928

Alan Sullivan with Will Rogers at Coronation
Gulf—July 1936

Sullivan Family at Tilford House (home of Basil and Kathleen Liddell Hart)—1946—after Alan and Bessie Sullivan returned to England from Canada following the war

Standing left to right: *Francois and Natalie Coulet, Basil and Kathleen Liddell Hart, Matthew Barry Sullivan, Bessie Sullivan, Alan Sullivan, Khom and Michael Sullivan, D'Arcy Sullivan*
Seated, left to right: *Judith and Jennifer Nelson (Kathleen's daughters)*

Acknowledgements

The assistance of the Canada Council by means of a research grant is gratefully acknowledged. I wish to thank the members of the family of the late Alan Sullivan for permission to quote from his writings and correspondence, and Barry Sullivan for permission to use his book *And Then We Went*. This book has been published with the help of a grant from the Canadian Federation for the Humanities, using funds provided by the Social Sciences and Humanities Research Council of Canada.

Preface

My interest in Alan Sullivan began in Sault Ste. Marie, when I was
a child. My parents spoke of Alan Sullivan, who had lived in Sault
Ste. Marie in the "early days" and had written about those days in
his novel, *The Rapids*. The stories of the filming of that novel, and
the presence in the city of the star, Mary Astor, fanned my interest.
As I became interested in Sullivan as an author, and as I read his
novels and short stories, I began to ask why, with very few
exceptions, the Canadians with whom I spoke about Sullivan did
not know who he was. I found this surprising because Sullivan had
published two books of poetry, a book of aphorisms, forty-two
volumes of fiction, a history of aviation in Canada 1917-18, at least
one translation of a Canadian novel written in French, and hundreds of short stories and articles, many of which had received wide
recognition. Of course, this situation did not apply only to Sullivan; when I first started serious research on the life and writing of
Charles W. Gordon, "Ralph Connor," in the early 1960s, I was
regarded as one committing literary suicide. Even fifteen years
ago, when I wrote my M.A. thesis on Frederick Philip Grove, that
name which is now setting up literary shock waves was not a
household word.

When I was working on the Ralph Connor papers, I realized
that the two men, Sullivan and Connor, had many things in
common: each had published over forty volumes; each had enjoyed
considerable success, but thirty years after the death of Connor,
and twenty years after the death of Sullivan, their names were
disappearing from the literary scene in which they had been major
figures from about 1890 until the 1940s. In other ways their lives
and accomplishments were similar. Both reflected in their writings a strongly held personal vision of the meaning of life; in the

xxi

case of both writers that view struck responsive chords in the minds of the reading public; both suffered from neglect by our literary critics. In the case of Sullivan, I have been able to locate in Canadian journals only three articles, aside from book reviews, relating to Sullivan, and one of these was written by Sullivan himself. I decided that someone should attempt to reconstruct a record of Sullivan's life and writings before it was too late. Part of my motivation is based on my belief that, until recently, Canadians in general, and literary Canadians in particular, suffered from an inferiority complex about their culture and for some inexplicable reason decided that authors with the publishing success of a Connor or a Sullivan did not deserve literary recognition. What might have been the result if the English had felt the same way about Dickens? I do not know whether it is strictly a Canadian phenomenon or not, but this attitude of Canadian literary critics implied that a popular work of fiction and a literary work of fiction were mutually exclusive forms of writing. In speaking of Canadian critics one does have to remember that literary criticism itself in Canada was not outstanding, either as to quantity or quality, until the last few decades of our literary history.

It is true, of course, that much popular fiction does not have literary merit and may have a short life. This, I think, will prove to be very true with regard to some extremely popular books published during the last decade. But I do not believe that a corollary to this situation should be that no popular novel will last or be considered to have literary merit. A very slight fraction of published fiction anywhere in the world has any chance of survival. Walter Allen, noting that "in 1961 no fewer than 4,485 new works of fiction were published in Great Britain alone," states: "We need a word to distinguish between the market commodity . . . and the novel which was intended, at any rate by the author, as a work of art. . . . Perhaps a hundred of them were published in 1961."[1]

The few Canadian literary critics who existed in the earlier part of this century, in addition to adhering to the theory that what was popular could not be art, made serious mistakes in identifying certain books as having literary merit which by any objective critical standard prove to lack any genuine literary value. A classic

---

1 Walter Allen, *Reading a Novel* (London: Phoenix House, 1963), p. 13.

example of this sort of mistake concerns the novel *The Lily of Fort Garry*, by "Jane Rolyat"; the author's real name was E. Jean Taylor McDougall.

The story of her early success as it is told in the *Literary History of Canada* is fascinating:

> That [name] of "Jane Rolyat" (E. Jean McDougall) seems to have been completely forgotten. It is a legitimate piece of Canadian literary history, however, to record that in the early 1930's she was regarded as the chief hope of Canadian fiction. Her first novel, *The Lily of Fort Garry* (1930), was advertised by J. M. Dent and Sons as The Canadian Novel in the September, 1930 issue of the *Canadian Forum*, and the London reader's enthusiastic assessment of the manuscript was printed in full. The concluding paragraph of the assessment ran as follows: "The book has genuine beauty and charm. . . . Miss Rolyat may easily develop into an accomplished writer of English prose. There is every possibility that she may become the first Canadian novelist of importance . . . ."
>
> In June 1933, Dent took a full-page advertisement in the *Forum* to announce Miss Rolyat's second novel, *Wilderness Walls* (1933). *Wilderness Walls* was announced as the first of a trilogy, in which Miss Rolyat had captured "the stillness and beauty of our own north country", and excerpts were quoted from enthusiastic reviews in English newspapers. . . .
>
> The remaining books of the trilogy, incidentally, seem never to have appeared.
>
> The contemporary reader who, in the light of these assessments, goes back to *The Lily of Fort Garry* and *Wilderness Walls* hoping to discover forgotten masterpieces will be gravely disappointed. . . .
>
> The astonishing thing about these books, . . . is that reputable Canadian critics once took them seriously. Canadians in the twenties and thirties were so anxious to discover the great Canadian novel that they saw it in books which had no claim whatever to genuine literary distinction. At the same time they came very close to ignoring the few books, such as the novels of Grove and Callaghan, that did at least come within the striking distance of greatness.[2]

The most disturbing fact about the Jane Rolyat story is that her novel *The Lily of Fort Garry* was written after most of Ralph

---

2   Carl F. Klinck, *Literary History of Canada* (Toronto: University of Toronto Press, 1965), pp. 664-66.

Connor's novels, after Frederick Philip Grove's *Settlers of the Marsh*, *Our Daily Bread* and *The Yoke of Life*, after Salverson's *The Viking Heart*, after Martha Ostenso's *Wild Geese*, and worst of all, as has been mentioned, after the early Callaghan.

A full discussion concerning the history of literary criticism in Canada—pointing out its failure to recognize at times true literary art and at other times its incorrect identification of inferior work as art, coupled with a propensity to regard popular fiction as having no literary worth—although it might prove interesting, would be out of place in this assessment of Alan Sullivan. But if such a discussion were undertaken, it might very well reveal a lack of much serious literary criticism in Canadian writing. Rather than become involved in such a negative endeavour, and to better develop an approach to Sullivan, I will refer briefly to valuable contributions to Canadian critical thought by two creative writers: Frederick Philip Grove and Ethel Wilson.

In essays in his *It Needs to Be Said* and in other published and unpublished essays and addresses, Grove set forth in a fairly complete way his view of art and the role of the artist or writer. In these writings Grove claims that he should be considered a realist, and he begins his analysis of realism with the definition he found in Annandale: "the endeavour to reproduce nature or to describe real life just as it appears to the artist." The central point of his theory of realism is that realism is not objective. He believes that before a work of literature can be a work of realism, it must be a work of art and conform to the canons of art; in art the artist is an indispensable medium through which we see things. The camera and the gramaphone, according to Grove, are more reliable than the human eye:

> The essential point, however, is that neither interposes the inter-
> pretative strain which, in a work of art, is furnished by the artist's
> soul, neither in other words mirrors and evokes the emotional
> reaction. Camera and gramaphone see and hear things from the
> outside, as it were. The artist fuses and reproduces them from out
> of his soul. In order for anything whatever to become a fit subject
> for art, it must be reborn in the soul of the artist.[3]

Grove sees the realist writer as one who must concern himself with the presentation not of himself but of human life:

---

3   Frederick Philip Grove, *It Needs To Be Said* (Toronto: Macmillan, 1929), pp. 59-60.

xxv
Preface

---

the work of art can spring only from an intimate almost mystical fusing of the two things which are needed—a thing presented and a soul presenting—[the artist] will never step forward into the limelight as a person . . . . he ceases to be a realist who speaks through things and human figures whom he marshals about on his stage; he becomes the pedant who points his moral, be it with an ever so magic wand.[4]

Grove's second major point is that a work of art must mirror "a more or less universal human reaction to what is not I."[5] And Grove sees this universal response as a "tragic reaction of the human soul to the fundamental condition of man's life on earth."[6]

Central to Grove's theory of art are the ideas he expresses in the following:

Inasmuch as it is the aim of art to express a purely human reaction to the phenomena of life, irrespective of human idiosyncrasies, it may be said to destroy individuality and to fuse the common humanity inherent in us all in a primitive response to the outside world; it may be said to interpret us to ourselves—our feelings, our reaction to life; and to make the deepest in us, that which ordinarily remains unconscious or semi-conscious articulate.

Art, then, appealing as it does, not to me as of this country or this age, but to the primeval human being in me, is of no nationality, and of no time. The quality of the emotional reaction awakened and directed by art, necessarily depends on and is tinged by, the quality of life itself as it has been from the beginning of the world. That quality being inherent in the very conditions of our existence on earth, has not changed and cannot change, no matter how much our so-called progress has changed the inessentials.[7]

In writing of his view of art and the role of the artist, Grove made it very clear that the correct environment was of absolute importance to the artist. To "body forth" a universal response the artist had to be exposed to a primeval environment. Grove wrote of his search for this environment:

When I was a young man, an occasion had offered itself for me to cross Siberia: and I had done so; and it was that fact which implanted in me the desire to see Canada, especially the west of

---

4   Ibid., p. 61.
5   Ibid., p. 63.
6   Ibid., p. 63.
7   Ibid., pp. 84-85.

Canada; for I had a suspicion that Canada was in many respects similar to Siberia.

. . . .

    I remained in Canada because there was in me one urge more powerful than any other; the urge to express certain things: in other words to write. And what I have wanted to write about, had offered itself in this country.[8]

I am a Canadian by choice. I am a Westerner by choice. I am also one who, whether successfully or not, strives after beauty. . . . I was searching for an environment which would help me to express that individual, tragic reaction to life, the world, the universe—to God—which I felt to be alive within me. . . . What kept me in Canada, and more especially in the Canadian west was the fact that I found here more clearly than elsewhere the germs of such a new or distinctive shade in the generally tragic reaction of human souls to the fundamental conditions of man's life on earth.[9]

    I will attempt to prove that Alan Sullivan, in his best work, achieved many of the ideals postulated by Grove. Just as Grove needed the primeval environment of the virgin prairie, Sullivan needed the primeval environment of the Canadian north or the Canadian Rockies to evoke the best artistic response within him. When Sullivan used the primeval settings with which he had become so familiar, he responded in what Grove would have considered to be a universal fashion, and produced works of art. In his best work Sullivan would be considered a realist—especially with regard to Grove's requirement that the writer never step into the limelight. It is unfortunate that Hugh Maclennan failed to follow Grove's advice—the frequent intrusion in Maclennan's novels of impassioned sermonettes about Canadian nationalism and Calvinism will eventually weaken his literary stature. The characters created by Sullivan in his novels set in the primeval surroundings of Canada's North and West are realistic figures in their struggle for survival. It is worth remembering that Sullivan wrote about these isolated areas of Canada half a century before Farley Mowat.

    Ethel Wilson, like Grove, has also set out, in a quite explicit way, her views of what constitutes art and what she considers to be

---

8   Frederick Philip Grove, unpublished (untitled) lecture (University of Manitoba Library, Grove Collection, Box 22; no date).

9   Grove, *It Needs To Be Said*, p. 54.

the role of the artist. Her basic statement about the writer of fiction is quite clear: "Assuming that a potential writer of fiction has also the power of observation, that he has something that needs to be said or told, and a sort of osmosis, writing is an art very much to be learned by doing."[10] The key word in this statement is "osmosis," which implies that mysterious talent which gives the artist greater insight than the ordinary observer. Wilson comes very close to holding Grove's view of the artist as observer and interpreter: "We are aware of the flavour of the writer's personality. . . . Although we rarely find in great works an over-awareness of the writer's self."[11] The other essential elements in Wilson's theory emerge from her use of the words "synthesis and incandescence":

> There is a moment . . . within a novelist . . . when some sort of synthesis takes place over which he has only partial control. There is an incandescence and from it meaning emerges . . . a fusion occurs. . . . I am sure that the very best writing in our country will result from such an incandescence which takes place in a prepared mind where forces meet.[12]

Stated simply, Wilson feels that an artist should have that mystical perception which she calls "osmosis" and that this talent enables the writer to see through the obvious and superficial appearance of things. It brings about the synthesis within the writer's mind which results in what she describes as "incandescence." To me, this is very similar to Grove's statement about the "explosion" which occurred in his mind when the hero of *Fruits of the Earth* was first conceived. He tells us that one day he had observed a new settler in south Manitoba:

> The important thing was this. His first appearance, on top of the hill, had tripped a trigger in my imagination; he had become one with many others whom I had known, and an explosion had followed in the nerve centre of my brain. . . . A momentous thing had happened; the figure of Abe Spalding, central to the book, . . . had been born in my mind.[13]

I will attempt to show that Sullivan exhibits the characteristic Wilson describes as "osmosis"—in Sullivan's case a profound

---

10   Ethel Wilson, "A Cat Among the Falcons," in A. J. M. Smith (ed.), *Masks of Fiction* (Toronto: McClelland and Stewart, 1961), p. 26.
11   Ibid., p. 28.
12   Ibid., p. 29.
13   Frederick Philip Grove, *In Search of Myself* (Toronto: Macmillan, 1946), p. 260.

understanding of the mystery of primeval environments and those who struggle to survive in those lands. As a result certain works of Sullivan possess the quality Wilson calls "incandescence."

If I were to attempt to capture in a graphic way the primeval environments which inspired Sullivan, I would use certain paintings by Tom Thompson and the Group of Seven. Many of their paintings suggest the rugged isolated terrain, the stormy clouded skies, and the mysterious gloomy forests of the land north of the Great Lakes, just as Sullivan's writing captures the same vision. Thompson's *Black Spruce in Autumn*, or J. E. H. MacDonald's *The Lonely North*, or Frank Johnson's *The Dark Woods*, or A. Y. Jackson's *March Storm* could serve as backdrops for readings from Sullivan's *The White Canoe and Other Verse*, *The Crucible*, or *The Rapids*. Arthur Lismer's *Cathedral Mountain*, or Lawren Harris's *Isolation Peak* or Varley's *The Cloud, Red Mountain, B.C.*, in the same way, would complement Sullivan's *Cariboo Road*, *The Great Divide*, or *The Splendid Silence*. I can imagine Lawren Harris's *North Shore, Baffin Island* as a frontispiece for Sullivan's *The Cycle of the North* or *The Magic Makers*. The parallels between the work of the Group of Seven and that of Sullivan could be developed further, but the point to be made is that just as the paintings of the Group of Seven should be preserved as part of our Canadian heritage so should the writing of Alan Sullivan.

I have said that Sullivan, like Grove, needed a primeval environment to evoke the best artistic response within him, and I have also referred to an affinity between Sullivan and the Group of Seven in the environments captured in his writing and their painting. In Sullivan's *The Passing of Oul-I-But and Other Tales* these two concepts are clearly exemplified. In that book Sullivan includes the story "Consecrated Ground," which is about the Honourable John Selkirk, who takes young Jamie Peters with him when he leaves Scotland to live with his son in Canada:

> Jamie swung his arm eloquently. Behind him the river, split by a rocky pinnacle, rushed by in twin torrents of thunderous foam. All around him the forest marched to its brink, and the air was full of sweet tumult and the unfathomed mystery of untenanted places. "It's yon," he almost whispered. "It's got me and I would'na leave it."
>
> There was that in Selkirk which moved in response. He knew it and felt it too, this call that summoned so many of his countrymen to lonely lodges.

. . . .

The call was getting very clear now. In his quiet dogged way he was doing his best to answer. The barren lands stretched ahead, naked and forlorn—a country sheared of ease and comfort and delight. And ever as the barrenness increased, Jamie's soul stripped away the shell that encased it and came forth nakedly to meet it. The Musselburgh caddy was wiped clean out of him, he had become the primordial Celt.[14]

This passage dramatizes Grove's theory concerning the response of the human soul to the primeval; what happens to Selkirk and to Jamie in fiction is what happened to both Grove and Sullivan in their own lives. They both understood and wrote about the power of primeval nature to evoke such a response in the human soul. In addition, one can easily imagine many paintings by the Group of Seven which could illustrate this story.

When I began my research into the life and writing of Sullivan, I realized that it would be futile to work through the normal literary channels. Instead I wrote to Zena Cherry whose column "After a Fashion" in *The Globe and Mail* is read by those people most likely to remember Sullivan. Her mention of my project brought an immediate response and eventually led to my meeting the four living children of Alan Sullivan. Although I knew in broad outline of the literary accomplishments of Sullivan, and in less detail of his accomplishments as an explorer, prospector, engineer, and industrialist, it was only when I began uncovering the details of both lives that I became aware of the many questions about the man. This book is an attempt to bring those questions to light and to find answers to some of them. I frankly admit the difficulty I have had reconstructing the early life of Sullivan, partly, as I have mentioned, because he did not interest Canadian literary critics and they did not record anything about him for us. His four children have said they did not attach much importance to what he had written and, as a result, did not probe into the motivation for his writing. Sullivan was not the sort of person who took himself seriously enough to keep written records; it was only during the last few months of his life that he jotted down some memories of his early life. Given this absence of records, there will be errors with regard to some specific dates and geographical locations. In addition, there has been considerable

---

14 Alan Sullivan, *The Passing of Oul-I-But and Other Tales* (Toronto: J. M. Dent and Sons, 1913), pp. 228-29.

difficulty locating copies of Sullivan's books. There is no complete collection of his published works anywhere in the world. Unfortunately, his children did not collect them, and Canada has only recently started to think of preserving records of our literary history. This was not a new experience for me: when I wrote my Ph.D. thesis on one hundred years of Canadian prairie fiction, in several instances the only copies of Canadian novels in existence were in the British Museum. Much of this difficulty has been overcome for me by the persistent searching for books undertaken by Mrs. Virginia Taylor of Lakehead University Library.

The details of Sullivan's life and writing from the time of his marriage in 1900 are much more certain; this is, in large part, because of the good memory of his elder daughter, Lady Liddell Hart, who remembers much of this period herself and who listened to her mother's conversations, before her death in 1974, about the early years of her marriage. Barry Sullivan, fortunately, burst into print himself at the age of ten, and his two little books about the early years in Europe have been of tremendous help. Madame Coulet and Professor Michael Sullivan have also been most helpful in filling in gaps for me. I appreciate, more than I can express, their assistance to me in this project, and I hope that this book will succeed in shedding new light on their father and his writings.

Lakehead University   Gordon D. McLeod
1980

I

In Search of Alan Sullivan

Hero, Prophet, Poet,—many different names in different times
and places, do we give to Great Men . . . I confess, I have no notion
of a truly great man that could not be all sorts of men. The Poet
who could merely sit on a chair, and compose stanzas, would never
make a stanza worth much. . . . I fancy there is in him the Politi-
cian, the Thinker, Legislator, Philosopher;—in one or other degree, he could have been, he is all these.
                                        — Carlyle, *On Heroes and Hero Worship*

Alan Sullivan was a Canadian, perhaps the archetypal Canadian;
his life and his writings, which are almost mirror reflections of each
other, combine to present the image of a man whose essential
characteristics are those attributed to the Canadian character.
Rarely are so many of these distinctive elements found in the life or
the writing of one man. Looking at Sullivan's fiction, one finds
these essential elements: many dichotomies; indications of a quest
for the essential characteristics of man; love of solitude and especially of the wilderness of Canada; understanding of Canada's
native people; writing which is Canadian in setting and tone but
also is European in both; emphasis on the attempt to realize ideals
and dreams; images of contemporary man confined in a cage;
understanding of the responsibilities of great wealth and also the
problems of those who are the labouring class; discussion of the
Canadian identity. If one then looks at the life of Sullivan, one
finds all of these same characteristics. Found in a composite figure,

1

they could be defined as the essential Canadian character. The Canadian human condition has been described in terms of an Old Testament situation: man expelled from the Garden of Eden and not yet restored to paradise—a man in search of a dream of that paradise—a man caged, as it were, and seeking escape. The Canadian human condition also is seen as containing dichotomies: the English-French and the British-American, to mention only two. These are part of Sullivan's vision of life. Considerable attention has been drawn in recent writing to the Canadian human condition viewed as "survival" or "isolation"; in Sullivan's life and writings these, too, are strongly emphasized. If the concept of Canada as a people and nation in search of their own identity is valid, then here Sullivan is seen both in his writing and his life to have been, as he was in so many other ways, avant-garde.

A starting point in the search for the essential Sullivan might be to look at the apparent dichotomies, both external and internal, in the man and the writer. Although from his early life until his death he expressed a love of solitude and the Canadian wilderness, he spent a large part of his life mingling with a sophisticated European society. Although he identified with the native peoples of Canada and with labouring classes here and abroad, he was equally at home with the privileged and the rich; although he disliked having material possessions himself, he did strive after material wealth. For the first fifty years of his life he appeared to be completely devoted to his activities as an engineer, a prospector, an explorer, and, eventually, an industrialist, but after the age of fifty he devoted most of his energy to the part of him that was artist and poet. He was born and lived in Canada for many years, but he married a young woman who had been born and educated in the United States and who became a dedicated Angiophile. Together, they spent about twenty years in Britain and Europe. He accepted the solid British Victorian standards of life, but a man whom he admired more than any other was an early "ugly American," Francis Clergue. Sullivan was an active, athletic, strong man who chose as his bride a fragile, slightly crippled young woman who was completely unsuited to outdoor life. These dichotomies at work within Sullivan certainly contributed to the outpouring of fiction from his imagination.

A second approach to Sullivan is the identification of the major influences on his life and writing. It is obvious that in seventy-eight years he was exposed to many influences, but there are at least four key turning-points in his life. When his father accepted election as Bishop of Algoma in 1882, Sullivan, then fourteen, was wrenched from the life of Montreal and Chicago to the relatively isolated and rugged area of his father's diocese stretching west from Sault Ste. Marie to the border of Manitoba and north to Hudson's Bay. As a young boy and again as a young man he accompanied his father on his visitations through this diocese. It was then that was born in him the love of the west and north of Canada that remained with him and led him, at the age of seventy-five, to travel to the Arctic. A second influence, one closely related to his father's move to Sault Ste. Marie, was his introduction, in 1894, to Francis Clergue, the American entrepreneur who for a time lived at Bishophurst with the Sullivan family and later employed Sullivan in some capacity at the steel works in Sault Ste. Marie. His interest in Clergue was first shown clearly in the novel *The Rapids* (1920), which is a thinly disguised biography of Clergue, but it remained with him until his death, when he had just completed a biography of Clergue. The third major influence on Sullivan was his marriage to Bessie Salsbury Hees in 1900, after a whirlwind courtship. When he married her, he entered a society of wealth, elegance, and, perhaps, of materialism. It is difficult to understand why Sullivan throughout his later life seemed to be obsessed with the necessity of acquiring money: he frequently spoke of "his ship coming in"; he sought to have his books filmed or produced as plays. It could be that he was striving to compensate for his wife's affluence. Perhaps Sullivan resented the gift from his father-in-law of his first home in Rat Portage (now Kenora) and of his homes on Madison Avenue and in Wychwood Park in Toronto; perhaps he resented being subsidized for much of his life by his wife's considerable fortune. Or, perhaps, it is just another dichotomy in the life of Sullivan: the simple nature-loving poet competing within the man with the potential entrepreneur. Perhaps it was just a practical and typically Canadian urge to achieve a permanent home, because for much of his life after leaving Canada Sullivan and his family lived at first in numerous rented homes and in hotels, and then for fourteen years in a rented country home from which frequent trips were made.

The final major influence on Sullivan was the move in 1920 to England, a move brought about completely by his wife. Was this forced exile from Canada beneficial to Sullivan, or did it have the opposite effect? Did his wife's decision inhibit him for many years, until he returned at first in spirit and then in person to Canada? The move obviously benefited his four children. All four of his living children have had exciting and rewarding lives, which they might not have had without the English education, the English society in which they mingled, and the exposure to the cultural and intellectual atmosphere in which they grew up. Bessie Sullivan did place her children in a situation where the potential of each was highly developed. With the exception of the eldest, Lady Liddell Hart, the children are probably really English. Barry Sullivan, for example, had not returned to Canada since he left it in 1920 at the age of five until 1979, despite his father's urging him to see the land of his birth. But for Alan Sullivan the move may not have been in his best interests, although there will be those who could argue that without the opportunity he had in England to meet and talk with the well-known writers of the time, he might never have achieved the success he did with his later novels. Regardless of the wisdom of the move, it did influence much of his later writing with regard to setting, style, content, and theme.

This British influence was, of course, not new to Sullivan. Although he was born a Canadian, his early life in the rectories in Montreal and Chicago and in Bishophurst at Sault Ste. Marie was that of a typical British child. He was surrounded by British servants, a British way of life, and was sent to a British Public School, Loretto, near Edinburgh, for five years. Although he loved the wilderness around Rat Portage, he began his married life there with an English man servant and a maid—hardly the typical beginning for a young Canadian couple. As a young man he travelled to Europe and, on at least one occasion accompanied his father when the Bishop went to recover his health in Mentone in France for about a year. Nonetheless, during his twenty years in England he chafed under the restraints of British life and pined for the freedom of the Canadian wilderness. He felt caged in Kent: he longed to be in the Arctic. The move to England was the result of a swift decision made by his wife when he was prospecting in the Yukon. Perhaps he should not have given in to her decision. However, in all this it must be remembered that Alan Sullivan loved Bessie Hees from the time he met her in 1900 until his death in 1947, not just with an ordinary love but with a romantic zest which he continually expressed to her in letters, in telegrams, in poems, even to the point of having one book of poetry privately printed for her.

Throughout his life Sullivan sought isolation. Apparently it was necessary for him to isolate himself from his family and friends to write. But it was also part of Sullivan's belief that isolation was necessary for anyone. While living at Sheerland House in Kent for fourteen years, he frequently isolated himself in his sparsely furnished study. When he and his family spent winters on the Italian Riviera, he fled to the isolation of a tower at Portofino. Even earlier, he was isolated in the attic of a house in Edinburgh during his vacations from school, and when he left the University of Toronto after one year, he retreated to northwestern Ontario. In London he sought escape from his family at the Savage Club and even took separate lodgings from his family. This isolation is a dominant component in Sullivan's fiction. Tom, the halfbreed in "The Essence of a Man," was isolated, and Clergue or Clark in *The Rapids* was, in his own way, also isolated. The isolation of Sullivan was not just physical but also spiritual: according to his children he really never "let down the barriers."

Sullivan's isolation was at least partly responsible for his use of the pseudonym "Sinclair Murray" for many of his novels. Although one of Sullivan's children suggested that the pseudonym was taken because the books were "pot-boilers," and another that it was because his publisher, John Murray, felt he could not bring out so many books by the same author, the use of the pseudonym is clearly explained by Sullivan in a letter written in 1934 to Basil Liddell Hart, who later became his son-in-law:

> Sinclair Murray—my alter ego—saw the light when Sullivan was coming out pretty fast—say two a year—also he gave Sullivan the opportunity to air "in print" under another name certain moods to which Sullivan readers were not attuned: we get on very well together, sharing the same overdraft and . . . the money. The understanding is that Sinclair shall not write short stories.[1]

Although it may be true that the Sinclair Murray name was used partly at his publisher's request, it is probably also true that Sullivan welcomed the creation of a person with whom he could "let down the barriers."

---

1 Alan Sullivan, letter to Basil Liddell Hart, December 14, 1934 (in the author's files).

In all of his life and writing there is also the concept of the search as one of the essential elements of man. Sometimes it receives explicit statement, sometimes it is only implied. At times it is expressed in Conrad-like terminology as "the testing" of man, and at other times in a more Canadian way as "survival." In creating the characters of his stories, Sullivan presents a catalogue of characteristics that can be seen as essential to greatness, which he did not see as belonging only to the rich and powerful but also to the humble, for example, the strong Indians and Eskimos of much of his writing. Sullivan admired loyalty, resiliency, and strength and those who had the courage and fortitude to withstand adversity. His writings set forth a stoical acceptance of death and of the violence involved in the natural cyclic pattern as it affected both wildlife and man. He admired those who undertook honest work and in so doing achieved independence. And most of all, in those who did survive he saw a vision, a characteristic of the prophet. These characteristics of man, who is often presented as in solitude and in the face of challenges which are accepted without complaint, were to Sullivan the essence of man. Many of them emerged in Sullivan himself in the fascinating life which he lived; consequently, when one seeks to gain a clear picture of this enigmatic man, one has to look at both his life and his writing.

II

The Young Alan

1

Alan Sullivan was born on November 29, 1868 in Montreal, the son of the Reverend Edward Sullivan and Frances Mary Renaud. Edward Sullivan came to Canada from Ireland in 1858 and was ordained an Anglican priest in 1859. He first married Mary Hutchinson in 1860, and then Frances Renaud in 1866. Frances was the daughter of a Scottish mother who, having been left a widow, came to Canada with her young family, one of whom became an Anglican priest in Montreal and through whom Frances met Edward Sullivan. In addition to their eldest child, Alan, Edward and Frances Sullivan had four other children: Kathleen died in 1895 in Sault Ste. Marie from typhoid fever, which she contracted from Alan whom she had nursed through a bout of the same disease; Nora married Harold Atlee Flint, a cousin of Clement Atlee, British Prime Minister from 1945 to 1951; Beatrice for many years was Social Editor for the Toronto *Mail and Empire* and for a short time for *The Globe and Mail*; Archibald, whom the family considered a "black sheep," was born in 1885 in Sault Ste. Marie and at the early age of sixteen went to live in New York, where he died in 1919. At the time of his death he was considered one of "the most brilliant young poets that ever came to New York."[1] The year after Alan's birth, the family moved to Chicago

---

1 Edward Caswell, *Canadian Singers and Their Songs* (Toronto: McClelland and Stewart, 1925), p. 265.

where Edward Sullivan was Rector of Trinity Church. Shortly before his death, while in the Grand Hotel in Monte Carlo, Alan Sullivan jotted down in an exercise book some of his memories of this early life in Chicago. He remembered the Chicago fire of October 9, 1872, when he was allegedly carried into Lake Michigan by his coloured nanny since the rectory was threatened by the flames. The house on Wabash Avenue between Twelfth and Thirteenth Street was not destroyed, and it was used as a place of refuge for many whose homes had been destroyed in the fire.

Sullivan also wrote of his memories of the cable cars and of his visit to a power house where he was fascinated by "the spectacle of a giant fly wheel with black snakey cable snaking through a hole in the wall from nowhere—to nowhere."[2] He wrote, "looking back at my then impressions I think they coloured my future life. From that moment I wanted to be an engineer."[3] He also wrote of the many marriages which took place in the rectory and of "uninvited people sleeping everywhere, on the billiard table, under, even on the stairs."[4]

At the age of nine he was sent to school in Canada, to a small private school on the banks of the Thames near London, Ontario. His only comment about this school was that he hated it. In 1878 Edward Sullivan returned to Montreal to be Rector of St. George's Church, where he had started out as a curate. In 1882 he was elected as second Bishop of Algoma, and the family moved to Sault Ste. Marie to Bishophurst, the large stone house built there through the generosity of the Baroness Burdett-Coutts of England and Mrs. Wymyss Simpson, the wife of a relative of Sir George Simpson, Governor-in-Chief of all the Hudson's Bay Company's territories from 1826 until 1860. Wymyss Simpson, who was Algoma's first Member of Parliament, had built his own large home, Upton, in the 1860s. Both large stone houses are still standing close together in Sault Ste. Marie and are occupied. This move to Algoma at the age of fourteen was a major factor in determining Alan's future life. It introduced him to the undeveloped part of Canada and created in him a love of the wilderness; it also introduced him to Francis Clergue, whom he admired and attempted to emulate for the rest of his life.

---

2   Alan Sullivan, notes written in an exercise book in 1947, while Sullivan was in Monte Carlo. A copy is in the author's files.

3   Ibid.

4   Ibid.

The Young Alan

Alan and his mother, with his three younger sisters, arrived at Sault Ste. Marie on a wooden lake steamer from Collingwood in July 1882. He wrote of the arrival:

> That period is still very vivid—a great adventure, our brains charged with visions of painted Indians with scalping knives of infinite sharpness, lurking around Bishophurst in the dark o' the night, their war whoops splitting the silence before the gory business began and my incredible bravery in defending my mother and sisters. My modesty in waving aside every word of praise.[5]

He also wrote that after the clang of Montreal "it all looked like paradise."[6]

John Stevenson wrote of this period in the life of Alan Sullivan in *Saturday Night* of August 23, 1947, shortly after the death of Sullivan:

> A boyhood spent at Sault Ste. Marie where his father reigned as Anglican bishop over a vast diocese and often took his young son as companion on his episcopal visitations, made him a lifelong lover of the woods and lakes and streams. He used to tell how on one of those pilgrimages, about 1880, he got his first introduction to his friend, Bishop Renison, when the latter's father, the resident Anglican missionary at Nipigon, summoned out of a group of dusky children a stocky sun-tanned lad who was quite indistinguishable from his Indian playmates.[7]

To appreciate the influence on Sullivan of his father's election as Bishop of Algoma, it is necessary to have some understanding of the Diocese of Algoma as it was in 1882 and also of the type of activity in which Bishop Sullivan was forced to become involved in administering the work of the church in this huge undeveloped area. The Diocese commenced at the Severn River, ninety miles from Toronto, and extended north and west to the height of land beyond the Great Lakes area; it was largely wilderness, eight hundred miles in length and one hundred and fifty miles in breadth, most of it densely forested. In 1882, the railroad was completed only to Gravenhurst and Fort William at the extremities of the Diocese. I have some knowledge of what the country was like at that time. My paternal grandparents had

---

5   Ibid.
6   Ibid.
7   J. A. Stevenson, "Alan Sullivan, Poet, Engineer," *Saturday Night* 62 (August 23, 1947), 25.

moved to a farm near Bruce Mines, forty-five miles east of Sault Ste. Marie, in 1874. My father was born there in 1883. In 1876 my maternal great grandparents moved to the same area. My mother was born there in 1890. Both of my parents frequently told me of the isolation their families had to endure. There was no access to either the east or the west by road or rail. For supplies from the outside world they were dependent on the steamships that travelled the Great Lakes. This meant, of course, that in winter there was no communication at all with the outside world. Local travel was by horse-drawn vehicles, boat, snowshoe, or the like. This was the period which preceded the discovery of great wealth in the forests and mineral resources of the area. However, some were already aware of that potential wealth. The first shaft of the copper mine at Bruce Mines had been sunk in 1848; it was this mine which brought my father's family from the Red River to Bruce Mines. My grandfather raised a breed of small horses used in the mining operation. My mother's family was drawn to the area from Belgrave, Ontario, to become involved in lumbering. The real development of the area did not begin until the Canadian Pacific branch line reached Sault Ste. Marie in 1887. When Bishop Sullivan arrived in Sault Ste. Marie in 1882, he found that his predecessor, the first Bishop of Algoma, Bishop Fauquier, had worked out a schedule to cope with the isolated seat of the Bishop. From May to November he made his headquarters in Sault Ste. Marie and visited by water the Indian and white settlements on the Upper Great Lakes. During the remainder of the year he lived in Toronto and visited the eastern part of his diocese.

Bishop Sullivan followed this same schedule and also carried on the extensive work begun by Bishop Fauquier with regard to the Indian population. Fauquier's ambition had been to convert the Ojibways and to provide them with education. There were already established missions at Garden River, near the Sault, and at Sheguiandah, on the Manitoulin, when Fauquier became Bishop. He made considerable progress while he held office.

In 1874, Fauquier built a combination schoolhouse and chapel at Batchawana Bay on Lake Superior. He also opened a mission among the Indians at Lake Nipigon. In Sault Ste. Marie, in 1873, Fauquier founded the Shingwauk Indian Industrial Home for Indian boys and, in 1879, the Wawanosh Home for Indian girls.

When Bishop Sullivan inherited Fauquier's mantle, it is obvious that his son, Alan, at the impressionable age of fourteen was greatly influenced by his father's work with the Indians. In addition to the two residential schools in Sault Ste. Marie for Indian children, there was the large Garden River Indian Reservation just a few miles east of Sault Ste. Marie where there had been an Anglican Mission since 1832 and, since 1883, St. John's Church. It was in this church that the Longfellow family placed a stained glass window in memory of the author of the poem *Hiawatha* which was believed to have been inspired by Longfellow's visit to Sault Ste. Marie in 1854. In 1900 his daughter, Alice Longfellow, and her sisters, Mrs. Dana and Mrs. Thorpe, came from Boston to Kensington Point (east of Sault Ste. Marie) for the first presentation by the Indians of Garden River of the dramatized version of their father's famous poem.

On June 29, 1882, at the age of forty-nine Bishop Sullivan was consecrated Bishop of Algoma. He travelled by steamer to Sault Ste. Marie. Shortly after becoming Bishop, Sullivan, following his predecessor's footsteps, journeyed to Britain to raise funds. His efforts were particularly successful, probably because of his eloquence as a preacher and because of his impressive appearance, which appealed to affluent British women. His greatest need at this time was for a boat for his journeys on the upper Great Lakes. Bishop Fauquier had travelled in an open sailboat. Sullivan collected over $5,000 and purchased a yacht in Scotland; originally known as *Zenobia*, it had belonged to the "playboy" Prince of Wales, later King Edward VII. Sullivan called it *Evangeline* and learned to operate it himself. He made many trips on this yacht to missions around the Great Lakes.

During the summer of 1884 Alan accompanied his father on these voyages, as he did in succeeding summers. It was one of these trips that John Stevenson refers to in his obituary of Alan Sullivan. Sullivan's daughter, Lady Liddell Hart, has a small water-colour painting showing her grandfather sitting by a lake with several companions while in the background Indians can be seen carrying a canoe. The Bishop is wearing full clerical dress, black shovel hat, and gaiters. Lady Liddell Hart feels that the gaiters were probably excellent protection against the mosquitoes. She did wonder, however, what the Indians would have thought of his extraordinary costume in the wilderness.

Alan Sullivan's life in what he considered to be the "paradise" of Sault Ste. Marie was confined to the summers from 1882 to 1886, because in the fall of 1882 he was sent to Loretto School near Edinburgh, one of the most spartan public schools in Britain. The choice of school was probably that of his strong-willed Scottish mother. It was there that Alan was to become an excellent athlete and where he came under the influence of the famous Headmaster, Dr. Hely Almond.

Before looking at Sullivan's memories of this period of his life, it is necessary to point out that Alan Sullivan had not been raised as a typical young Canadian boy. He was reared as the eldest son would have been in a typical British upper-middle-class family home. He had nannies and governesses. He was never sent to an ordinary public school (Canadian terminology) but always to private schools. He and his younger brother and his three sisters all received most of their education in Britain. His home life—although some of it was spent in northern Ontario—was that of British rectory life. He was surrounded by good English furniture, silver, and books. There were always servants—in Montreal, in Chicago, in Sault Ste. Marie, and in Toronto. The homes of his parents until he was thirty-two years of age were large, well-appointed, and comfortable.

The intimate friends of the Sullivans in Sault Ste. Marie were the English or Anglophile citizens, not the more rugged descendants of the original pioneers, who had cleared the land and lived in log cabins. Alan was hardy, but not as a result of a pioneer upbringing—it came rather from the austere Scottish private-school pattern imposed upon him. Francis Clergue has written of young Alan's race from Bishophurst for an early morning dip in the St. Mary's River during the winter; this was the result of the British cold-shower syndrome, rather than from necessity; there were warm bathrooms in Bishophurst. It was a desire to escape to the wilderness that drove Alan in that direction in his life and writing, rather than an early experience of life in the wilderness. Like Grey Owl, who pretended to be an Indian as an adult and who succeeded in this hoax, Sullivan, too, may have wished to escape the imprisoning pattern of his youth. Incidentally, Sullivan said forty years before the hoax was exposed that he was sure that Grey Owl was not an Indian because of the way he walked.[8]

---

8   This comment by Sullivan was related to me by Barry Sullivan.

The Young Alan

2

Alan Sullivan spent four years at Loretto, from 1882 to 1886. In his jottings shortly before his death in 1947, he dwelt to some extent on the unhappiness of those early years away from home. He mentioned the arduous journey by ship across the Atlantic in 1882 in the company of Mrs. W., a martinet. He also wrote of his first impression of Hely Almond:

> ragged ginger beard, white flannel trousers, flannel shirt open at neck, sparkling blue eyes, no hat, shapeless shoes. Believed in good digestion, the classics, good plain food, plenty of exercise, as few clothes as possible. Loved youth.[9]

Musselburgh, the site of Loretto School, was on the Firth of Forth, six miles from Edinburgh and was described by Sullivan as "cold, damp, bleak, inhospitable, windswept from the North Sea."[10] The young adolescent Alan, as soon as Mrs. W. left him, thought of escape—running away; the harsh setting of the school did not appeal to him. He was terribly conscious at that time of being undersized as a result of what he termed "a bout of malaria in childhood."[11] He felt that his clothing was out of place and that he was skinny. On reflection, in old age, he thought about the sacrifice that his parents must have made to send him to school at such a great distance. All he could think of then was being alone in Scotland in the care of the dour Mrs. W., four thousand miles away from home.

He then writes of his attempts to impress his schoolmates with his stories of Chicago: the great fire, the Great Lakes, the Indians. But he found that they were more interested in the scars left from mosquito bites and even more in football! This of course became the common interest. By the time he left Loretto, Alan was a good athlete and, apparently, an excellent football player. This was to stand him in good stead on his entrance, later, to the University of Toronto, but would also lead to his early departure from that university. One can easily imagine the harshness of the surroundings of this most spartan of schools. Even now, to an outsider, the British Public School environment seems forbidding, but in 1882 it must have been horrifying. He makes mention in his

---

9   Alan Sullivan, exercise book, 1947.
10   Ibid.
11   Ibid.

notes of the bare room with five other boys and of the windows with wooden shutters which did not close properly, and the bath which was pushed under the bed. He talked of being forced to participate in the "fagging system"[12] for the first two years, when he had to clean football boots, make toast, and do anything else demanded of him by the senior students. He even had to caddy for them when they played golf.

He was later astounded at the ignorance of British students about Canada; they pictured him wearing furs and cutting down pine trees to make firewood throughout the year. They thought that Canadians had to be constantly armed to ward off the attacks of the Indians. He wrote, "I disliked their confident air and the suggestion of superiority in their voices—and they had horses for polo in the holidays."[13]

Alan's Christmas holidays were a nightmare; they were spent in Edinburgh at the home of Mrs. W. in Drumshough Gardens, one of a row overlooking a cab stand. He wrote of his room "up four flights, bare, no fireplace. A few books, mostly biographies of Scottish divines. One front window. Sometimes played on the street."[14] He complained, "I was not taken to any theatre but to church to hear a sixty minute sermon."[15] He then writes of putting in time by climbing the Sir Walter Scott monument as many as four times in a day. One incident not included in his own written memories of these days at school was earlier related to his children. By some means he had got possession of an early air rifle, and for a time he amused himself by shooting out of the attic window. Unfortunately, an irate neighbour traced the trajectory of a pellet which had broken a window in his home and the culprit was apprehended. One can imagine the result of that discovery on poor Alan!

3

In 1886, at the age of eighteen, Alan returned to Sault Ste. Marie. That autumn he entered the School of Practical Science at the University of Toronto in Civil Engineering. Although the various

12 Ibid.
13 Ibid.
14 Ibid.
15 Ibid.

obituaries written about Sullivan on his death in 1947 and other printed records list him as a graduate of the University of Toronto, this is not so; in actual fact, at the beginning of his second year, in the fall of 1887, he suffered a severe concussion during a football game and left the university. He spent the next few years in northern Ontario, where he regained his health and started on an amazing career as an engineer, a prospector, an explorer, and a writer. It was during those years that he wrote the poetry which was published in 1891 and 1893.

Although Sullivan's injury brought an abrupt end to his formal education, it came at a time when opportunities had begun to open up in the Diocese of Algoma and other remote areas of western and northern Canada. When one looks back at his accomplishments in the areas of engineering and geology and remembers that his formal education in these fields covered only a single academic year, one must remember that in that period of Canadian history it was not unusual for men without formal education to rise rapidly in business and industry. The situation in the Diocese of Algoma by the end of 1887 had changed considerably since the arrival of the Sullivan family in 1882, when settlement in the Algoma Diocese was limited to areas easily reached by steamers.

The opening up of the area began as the railway was extended first to North Bay, in 1882, and, finally, when it joined the railroad built east from Port Arthur in 1885. As I said before, the Canadian Pacific branch line reached Sault Ste. Marie in 1887. Other shorter branch lines were added as well, and as the railway network extended, so did the settlement of the area. This, of course, created a need for clergymen to minister to the railroad builders and the settlers who followed them. While this caused recruiting problems for Bishop Sullivan, it created opportunities for the Bishop's son, Alan Sullivan.

Soon after leaving the University of Toronto, Alan was employed by the Canadian Pacific Railway, first as a member of one of the several geological survey crews the railroad set up to investigate the mining possibilities on the vast holdings of land they had acquired along the right-of-way of the railroad. Eventually, Sullivan became the leader of one of these geological exploration crews; he also managed to use his engineering skills by becoming a construction superintendent on one of the branch lines of the Canadian Pacific. At this time he was a strong young man, about five feet eleven inches tall, with a full brown beard and piercing bright eyes. There are many photographs of him in front of the tents and cabins which were, for several years, his homes. It was this period which gave birth to some of his best fiction. In an address delivered in England many years later, Sullivan referred to those early years between 1887 and 1892:

> By profession I was for many years an engineer and explorer in Northern Canada. I am a Canadian. My life, during those years, meant for long periods what is described as solitude so far as my own kind were concerned. My companions were mostly primitives. But now, looking back at these years, it seems that perhaps they helped to stimulate the action, or at any rate the life of certain compartments of the mind, which in surroundings of what we are pleased to term civilisation, function with considerably more difficulty. That is my experience. May I suggest to you that the thinking man need never feel alone. The opportunities of mental seclusion become the more precious with the increasing complexity of modern life.
>
> The colour of such an existence as I formerly led was surprisingly definite. One's body inured to effort and exercise, worked automatically. One was hardly conscious of it. One's mind appeared to develop from within. As Browning puts it "creased consciousness lay smooth". Being, as it were, a creature of nature, governed primarily by natural processes and changes, one became more receptive. One stretched, so to speak, a mental aerial, and because there was no local interference, seemed to catch vibrations otherwise lost. One was conscious of atmosphere, that curious condition of receptivity, a condition which I believe to be primarily negative, because it means only the absence of things that interfere.
>
> As to mental fodder, one seemed to need but little. One largely supplies oneself. But I remember one winter when my library consisted of Sidney Smith's "Wit and Wisdom", "Marcus Aurelius", "Lorna Doone" and I tramped across the wilderness day after day chanting Wordsworth's "Ode on the Intimations of Immortality" to a band of thoroughly mystified Cree Indians.[16]

Sullivan's daughter, Lady Liddell Hart, tells an interesting anecdote about this early period in her father's life. She mentions that

---

16   Alan Sullivan, typescript of an address delivered (ca. 1935) to a women's organization in England which he referred to as "The League" and which was presided over by Mrs. Dawson Scott (in the author's files).

in his capacity as the leader of a C.P.R. geological survey crew he "was allowed to flag trains to stop, and once, at the end of a very arduous time in the wilderness, and being lost for a time, he boarded a passenger train—very bearded, tattered clothes, starved. The people in the dining car look terrified when he came in and sat at a table. The menu was given him; he asked for dry sherry and olives to start with. His fellow travellers relaxed—the wild man must be civilised after all." She also tells of one experience he related to her about his work as a construction superintendent on a spur line of the railroad. "Father was a great lover of trees and showed us on a map where the railway curved. This, he explained, was because he wanted to save some magnificent trees."

As has been mentioned, it was during these years spent in hard physical work, while living in the most primitive conditions, often with Indians as his companions, that Alan Sullivan wrote the poetry which resulted in his first two published books, the first of which was a slim volume of verse, *The White Canoe and Other Verse* (1891). It, like Sullivan himself, is somewhat of a mystery. None of his four children has ever seen it. The book itself is almost impossible to locate, but there is a copy in the Victoria College Library, at the University of Toronto. The sixteen poems are varied and only a few are intimately related to the northern setting in which they were conceived. The first poem, "The White Canoe," and the last, "Farewell to the White Canoe," are obviously appropriate. The second, entitled "A Vision," is to a sweetheart, and two later ones—"The Widower's Lullaby" and "Lullaby"—are about a young man whose young wife had died leaving him with an infant. "Supposing" is also a love poem. No explanation has been found as to their inspiration; obviously they were not written to or about Bessie Sullivan whom Sullivan did not meet for another nine years. The poem "Confession, Creed and Prayer" reflects his close connection with the church. "To My Pipe" and "To My Indian Pipe" are quite whimsical. The most interesting poem in the volume, "A Song of Life," is Sullivan's vision of the future, in which he sees himself fifty years hence. To add to the mystery of this volume, Sullivan, in a letter written in 1931 to J. D. Logan of Toronto, suggests that he no longer has a copy of this first volume of poetry; in the letter he also expresses some thoughts about youthful inspiration:

> I sent you today a copy of a booklet of verse published when I was somewhere in the twenties [*Venice and Other Verse*] and have looked

in vain for a copy of one still earlier. Perhaps it is as well that it cannot be found. The perusal of this verse wakens memories of that divine flush of feeling which I suppose can only come to youth. That is where one pays for experience in a certain loss of ecstatic sensitive responsiveness . . . . No words or colour or rhythm can ever compensate for the lack of it.[17]

In the poem that gave the first volume of verse its title, "The White Canoe," Sullivan expressed a typically Canadian theme:

> So come when the moon is enthroned in the sky
>> And the echoes are sweet and low
> And nature is full of the mystery
>> That none but her children know.
> Come, taste of the rest that the weary crave
>> But is only revealed to a few:
> When there's trouble on shore, there's peace on the wave
>> Afloat in the White Canoe.[18]

More than fifty years later, following a successful career as a writer of novels and short stories, he returned to poetry, to Canada, and to himself:

> Now before the very end of the Portage, I lower my shoulder to
>> dump the familiar load
> Where it takes no harm, make fire with a curl of yellow bark where
>> a ragged old birch trunk
> Offers its friendly parchment, and, in the manner of a woodsman
>> after a variegated day,
> Consider not the morrow, but what lies dwindling behind me,
>> with my back to a tree.[19]

These lines are from a long unpublished poem written just before his death which he called "To My Children—A Parental Whimsy." Sullivan began his writing career with poetry, and after a long period of fiction returned, before his death, to poetry. Sullivan's first writing reflected the wilderness of Northern Canada and he ended on the same note.

Venice and Other Verse, published in 1893, when Sullivan was twenty-five, is a much more conventional selection of poems:

---

17 Alan Sullivan, letter to J. D. Logan, June 5, 1913 (in the author's files).
18 Alan Sullivan, *The White Canoe and Other Verse* (Toronto: Bryant Co., 1891), p. 1.
19 Alan Sullivan, "To My Children—A Parental Whimsy." Unpublished. A copy is in the author's files.

several of them reflect a solid British education in the poetry of the Romantic Period and earlier. However, at least one of them, "A Trapper's Death," captures the mood of another poet experienced in the north, Duncan Campbell Scott:

> Here in the peace of the deep woods' breast
> A worn old huntsman takes his rest,
> With naught but the wash of the wandering stream,
> And the sign of the wind through the maples' crest,
> As the monotone of his endless dream.[20]

After these two little volumes were published there is a gap of almost twenty years in Sullivan's writing career. This situation is explained to a certain extent by Sullivan in an article he wrote about himself for the *Ontario Library Review* and published in November 1929. It is always rewarding to find such a piece of writing in which an author has frankly attempted to assess his own contribution to literature. Sullivan's article, "In The Matter of Alan Sullivan," has greater candour than most:

> The next twenty years or so passed with but some transient verse and no prose. One was too hard at work, and getting, unconsciously, innumerable and varied experiences which, I suppose, in a cumulative fashion finally determine one's characteristics and points of view. My work was in the north and far north. I lived out of doors, my home being a tent. Railways, ship canal surveys, explorations for timber and minerals, the development of mines, investigation of potential waterpower, lumbering, contracting, these were the activities that occupied me till a turn of the wheel found me as chief engineer of a large manufacturing works.
>
> The change was abrupt, my duties were confined, arduous, exacting and mechanical, and I very soon found myself in danger of developing the technical side of my brain while a sort of intellectual dry rot took possession of its other portion. To counteract this I acquired the habit of having every night, a mental house cleaning. For two or three hours I forgot mechanics, devoted myself to fiction and encouraged in every possible way an endangered faculty of imagination. It meant considerably reduced hours of sleep, but it seemed worthwhile.
>
> Books began to appear, beginning with the "Passing of Oulibut," a collection of short stories mostly of the north. Then came "The Inner Door," which dealt with the point of view of thinking employees in a large works and the conflict of interests

---

20   Alan Sullivan, *Venice and Other Verse* (Toronto: Bryant, 1893), pp. 39-42.

which so often creates a regrettable gulf between master and man. After that "Blantyre-Alien." This was really more of a character study than a novel, depicting the inner conflicts which take place when a man of strong feelings and impulses adopts a type of life and surroundings which are foreign to his nature.[21]

In 1892 Alan Sullivan's employment with the Canadian Pacific was brought to a temporary conclusion by his father's failing health. By that year, Bishop Sullivan had served Algoma for ten years. But the heavy travel schedule and the fund-raising efforts had affected his health. In September 1892 he had a nervous breakdown. The Diocese of Algoma granted him $1,500 for travel for one year. Accompanied by Alan, the Bishop went to Europe where he stayed at Menton on the Mediterranean. This stay on the French Riviera probably gave birth to the love Alan Sullivan felt for the Mediterranean during the European part of his life. Years later he was to write some of his books in "The White Tower" on the cliff overlooking another part of the Riviera, Portofino.

The Bishop attempted to resume his duties in August 1893, but he was soon ill again. Alan accompanied his father to Colorado for a rest, and returned with him to Sault Ste. Marie, where the Bishop was able to carry out his duties only a few months at a time between relapses. While Alan Sullivan was at home in Bishophurst in Sault Ste. Marie in 1894, there arrived in the city the now famous entrepreneur, Francis Clergue, who brought a new, major influence into Sullivan's life.

In order to understand the depth of Sullivan's later involvement with Clergue and the possible reasons for it, it is necessary to give in some detail the outline of Clergue's career. When he first arrived, Clergue stayed in Sault Ste. Marie, Michigan under an assumed name. A week later he moved to the Algonquin Hotel in Sault Ste. Marie, Ontario. At the end of that week, on October 1, 1894, he concluded his negotiations with the Ontario town of 4,000 by agreeing to purchase a power canal and small power house built by the town, which had to sell the company because of financial problems. The agreement was the first step in the founding of Clergue's industrial empire which finally included, among others, Lake Superior Power, Michigan Lake Superior Power, Algoma Steel, International Transit, Sault Ste. Marie Pulp and

---

21   Alan Sullivan, "In the Matter of Alan Sullivan," *Ontario Library Review* 14 (November, 1929), 35.

Paper, Tagoma Water and Light, Algoma Central and Hudson
Bay Railway. This complex of industries grew from the parent
Clergue Company, Consolidated Lake Superior Company. In 1902
and 1903, a New York financial group reorganized the companies
and forced Clergue's resignation following riots in Sault Ste. Marie
resulting from the companies' inability to pay their employees. In
1907 another legendary figure, James Dunn, later Sir James
Dunn, whose destiny was later linked to Algoma Steel, helped
Clergue to interest the English financier, Robert Flemming, in the
floundering Lake Superior Corporation. It was at this point in his
life that Clergue finally left Sault Ste. Marie. In his introduction to
a new edition of *The Rapids* in 1972, Michael Bliss, an historian at
the University of Toronto, writes about Clergue:

> *The Rapids* recaptures the period in our national development when
> businessmen were the "national class," the men who were building
> a nation by driving steel through the wilderness . . . . It was the
> period when a writer could discuss the tasks facing the Canadian
> "people" and define that group as "the capitalists, the bankers, the
> businessmen," and—as an afterthought—"the other classes."
> These were the years when men in business were building the
> Canadian nation, or were thought to be.
>
> . . . .
>
> Francis H. Clergue (Robert Fisher Clark in *The Rapids*)
> compiled a spectacular record of failure in his early business career.
> In 1880 as a young lawyer in Bangor, Maine, he did launch the
> town's electric street railway, the first in his state. From that
> beginning he proceeded to lose all of his backers' money in an
> electric light and power station on the Penobscot River . . . .
> Moving on to greater things, Clergue began negotiations with the
> Shah of Persia looking towards the construction of the first trans-
> Persian railway. United States Secretary of State James G. Blaine
> was among the backers of his Persian Railway and Construction
> Company, Persian Electric Light Company, and City of Teheran
> Water Works. . . . Back in Bangor he promoted several mining
> companies that all failed, and finally ran out of credibility when he
> proposed a massive power development involving damming and
> diverting the Penobscot. Then he came to Canada.[22]

For many years after he left the city, not much was known about
Clergue, especially in Sault Ste. Marie. All that remained in the

---

22 Michael Bliss, Introduction to Alan Sullivan, *The Rapids* (Toronto: Uni-
     versity of Toronto Press, 1972), pp. vii-viii.

1930s was the crumbling mansion, Montfernier, on Moffley Hill, stories of the parties in the house and on his sumptuous sixty-foot yacht, *Siesta*, and the occasional anecdote about his private life. In 1937, when he was invited back to Sault Ste. Marie to be presented with a portrait of himself, it was learned that he was still rich and at the head of a company called Universal Engineering Corporation. The source of the wealth on which he lived for the rest of his life was unknown until Dr. Donald Eldon[23] solved the mystery while doing research at Harvard University on Canadian entrepreneurs. Apparently, during the First World War, when he was selling armaments in Europe, Clergue made a large sale to the Russian Imperial Army. The shipment was lost in a fire, but it was insured, and the manufacturer was paid by the insurance company. By this time the Russian Revolution had occurred, and there was no Russian Imperial Army. Clergue kept the money which he had received from the Imperial Army. It may have been information like this that would explain why the manuscript of Sullivan's biography of Clergue, which was written just before Sullivan's death, was missing for many years after it was sent to the last survivor of the Clergue family. That missing biography is now in the possession of Professor Bliss.

Shortly after Clergue moved into the Algonquin Hotel he was invited, along with his brother Bernard, to be the guest of The Right Reverend Dr. Edward Sullivan, Lord Bishop of Algoma, in his home, Bishophurst. It was then that Alan, aged twenty-six met Clergue and shortly after was employed by him to work at the Lake Superior Company. It is not difficult to understand why Sullivan would be impressed by Clergue, for within a few years the man had built a hugh industrial complex and, although obviously not on solid foundations, an impressive financial empire. At the peak of this part of Clergue's career he built his fabulous mansion and entertained members of international society, including royalty. That was a very heady diet for an impressionable young man in the small community of Sault Ste. Marie in the 1890s. In 1929 Sullivan wrote about Clergue:

---

23   Dr. Donald Eldon, former Vice-President of Lakehead University, was the author of "The Career of Francis H. Clergue," *Explorations and Entrepreneurial History* 3 (April, 1951), 254-68. He related the information about the source of Clergue's final fortune in a private conversation.

After that came "The Rapids." This book was really a tribute to a man under whom I worked and for whom I have always had the greatest admiration. The story was cast in a town called St. Marys, the place really being Sault Ste. Marie, and deals with certain events which took place there. The hero was a prophet, in other words, he was a man with one great idea, one magnificent ambition, which naturally possessed him. His was the case of the dreamer who sees the perfect work stretching before him, who flings himself into it with splendid devotion, but to whom it is not given to bring about the ultimate fruition of his dreams. Canada owes more than most of us imagine to men of this type, and, very generally, the profits of the commercially successful are built on the shattered dreams of others.

A film was made of this story, but I have never seen it.[24]

By 1896 Sullivan had again become involved in prospecting and exploration in the area around what is now Kenora, Fort Francis, and Rainy River. In 1896 his father had resigned as Bishop of Algoma because of failing health and had been appointed Dean of St. James Cathedral, Toronto, a position he held until his death three years later in 1899. After 1896, when Sullivan left the employ of Clergue, he was again living in tents. One interesting item remains from this year. Sullivan made a long piece of letter paper out of birch bark on which he wrote a poem, and also made a complete envelope out of birch bark, and mailed them to his sister Nora, who was at school at Hamilton House, Tunbridge Wells, England. The postmark of the destination is very clear but, unfortunately, the Canadian one is not. This piece of memorabilia is fascinating because it is the sort of thing that turns up much later in his fiction about the Canadian west and north. For example, in *The Magic Makers* much of the plot depends on a letter written on hide and sent from the Arctic to Edinburgh. By 1898 Sullivan was in England attempting to find financial support for his mining ventures. There are in existence letters from Bishop Sullivan to his son wishing him well in this venture. One of these, dated December 14, 1898, refers to their mutual sadness over the death of the beloved Kathleen, Alan's sister. Bishop Sullivan died himself less than a month later on January 6, 1899. Alan was not in Toronto for the funeral.

Only a limited portion of this book is devoted to Sullivan's parents, not because they were not an important factor in his life,

---

24   Alan Sullivan, "In the Matter of Alan Sullivan," p. 35.

but, as with the lives of Alan's own children, if one were to treat them in detail, the work would grow into several volumes and would lose its focus on Alan Sullivan. However, one anecdote might throw more light on the character of the Bishop, who was a large, bluff man with a good Irish sense of humour. He was obviously a man of great strength and certainly of immense popularity. Apparently, in the last few years of his life, St. James Cathedral was usually filled to overflowing to hear his sermons. While he was in Sault Ste. Marie, he hosted the visit of an Anglican Evangelist from England who, towards the end of his visit, at a public gathering remarked: "I attended a delightful afternoon tea with the members of the Women's Missionary Society, but how many souls were saved? I attended a delicious supper with the members of the Men's Club, but how many souls were saved? I attended a meeting of the Vestry at which much business was done, but how many souls were saved?" Bishop Sullivan is alleged to have stood up and replied, "I turn to The Gospel According to Saint John, Chapter 2, and read of Christ attending a marriage feast in Cana of Galilee where he turned water into wine, but how many souls were saved?"

After the death of Bishop Sullivan, his wife Frances wore floor-length dresses of unrelieved black for the rest of her long life. She lived with her daughter Beatrice, in Toronto until she was almost one hundred years old, and was a familiar figure who was always described as the "Widow Sullivan" when she went down the aisle of St. James Cathedral. A well-known portrait of her painted by Archibald Barnes shows her to have been a tall, stately woman of somewhat severe expression. Although she bore a French name, she was actually a Scotswoman, both in birth and personality. The Renaud ancestors had emigrated from Switzerland to Scotland generations earlier. When one looks at her portrait, one cannot but think that she would have had considerable influence on the life of her eldest son. She did make visits to him and his family after they moved to England, and was known affectionately as Grannie Sullivan. It is significant that the second last book published by Sullivan, *"And From That Day,"* was dedicated "To the unfading memory of My Mother." The book is a fictionalized account of the crucifixion.

III

The Family Man in Canada

1

When Alan Sullivan reached the age of thirty, in 1898, he was unmarried, and relatively unsuccessful in the various careers he had followed. He must have been frustrated by his situation in life; for thirty years he had lived surrounded by wealthy and influential people, but he was himself without any wealth and with very little prospect of acquiring any.

Alan's father Edward had been the son of a poor Irish Wesleyan minister. Edward had emigrated from Ireland to the Diocese of Huron, in Ontario, where he was ordained a priest in the Anglican Church by Bishop Cronyn in London, Ontario in 1859. Edward's skill as a preacher brought rapid promotion within the church, from one rich parish to another, the first of which, St. George's in Montreal, was one of Canada's leading Anglican churches. From Montreal he went to the prestigious Trinity Church in Chicago. In 1879 he returned to St. George's, Montreal as Rector. After serving as Bishop of Algoma from 1882 until 1896, he became Rector of St. James Cathedral, Toronto. In this position he ministered to the leading Anglican congregation in Canada. In all of these positions, Bishop Sullivan and his family mingled with rich and influential members of Canada's "Establishment." But at no time was there any opportunity for the Bishop to accumulate money.

It must be remembered that in the 1880s and 1890s the Anglican Church of Canada was very powerful and that the congregations in Montreal and Toronto were made up of those who inhabited the ornate Victorian mansions of the two major cities in Canada. It was during this period that Jarvis Street in Toronto, for example, was a tree-lined avenue of huge sandstone and brick mansions, in which lived the most powerful people in Ontario. Even when Bishop Sullivan lived in what was then the remote community of Sault Ste. Marie, he maintained winter quarters in Toronto and travelled frequently on fund-raising and preaching missions to Europe, where as an Anglican Bishop he was welcomed into the homes of the aristocracy of the British society. Alan, while at Loretto School in Scotland, was taken to some of these homes by his father, and later he accompanied the Bishop on some of his trips to England; in 1892 he spent almost a year with the ailing Bishop at Menton, one of the most fashionable resorts in Europe.

In addition to the contacts Alan made with the rich and influential in Canada and Britain, there was his acquaintance with Clergue, the man who epitomized the successful nineteenth-century entrepreneur. It is not surprising that by the age of thirty Alan Sullivan wished to become a member of that influential part of society of which he had been an observer for his entire life.

On the death of Bishop Sullivan, not only was there no inheritance for Alan, but he had to assume some of the responsibility for his mother and unmarried sister. It has to be remembered that Alan's mother, Frances Renaud, had no money of her own. After the Bishop's death in 1898, for the first time since her marriage, Mrs. Sullivan was not provided with a large home by the Anglican Church, and she was forced to live in a small apartment in Toronto. She was able, however, to spend long periods of time in England with her youngest daughter, Mrs. Harold Atlee Flint.

I believe that Alan Sullivan, during the years when he sailed with his father on the yacht *Evangeline*, or mingled with the rich at Menton or in Britain or Toronto, and when he worked with the colourful Francis Clergue, grew increasingly ambitious to become one of those people instead of what he was: a poor young man with only one year of university education. I believe, as well, that in the late 1890s Alan Sullivan set out to capitalize to the utmost on all the connections with the rich that he had made during the first thirty years of his life. There is strong evidence to support this belief.

During the years following his leaving the University of Toronto, Sullivan had become very familiar with the area of

Ontario north and west of Sault Ste. Marie. He had worked for the Canadian Pacific Railroad as leader of both exploration and construction crews and had become knowledgeable about the mineral wealth buried in the rocks of Northern Ontario. As was mentioned earlier, after leaving active employment with Clergue, Sullivan had returned to those areas and used his experience to find mineral resources which could be developed to make his fortune. But he needed financial backing. It was this need which took him to England in the late 1890s and kept him there through the last illness and death of Bishop Sullivan.

Alan Sullivan was successful in gaining the support he needed. The Anglo-Canadian Gold Estates, Limited, was registered on August 1, 1899. By that time, of the authorized capital of 61,000 pounds in shares with a par value of one pound each, 52,635 shares had been issued. The purpose of the company was to carry on exploration and development and to acquire from the Rat Portage Lumber Company, Limited, the right of prospecting and of acquiring mineral lands on about 157 square miles (later increased to 200 square miles) in the Lake of the Woods and Rainy River Districts of Ontario. By the time the company was registered, Sullivan had negotiated the acquisition of these lands for 5,000 pounds in cash, 16,000 fully paid ordinary shares in the new company, and 200 pounds in fully paid deferred shares.

All of the financing for the new company was British, and the Head Office was in London, England, where F. Denvers-Summers, Secretary of the company, looked after the business from that side of the Atlantic. The Canadian office was in charge of Alan Sullivan, who by that time had assumed the title of Civil and Mining Engineer. The first Canadian office was in Rat Portage, but it was later listed as being in Port Arthur, although by that time Sullivan was acting as manager of the Elizabeth Mine and living at the mine. The major shareholders in the company and its directors were S. W. Paddon (Chairman), R. J. Price, Esq., M.P., Thomas Greenwood, and W. E. Wimpenny, Esq.

2

After completing the arrangements for the establishing of the Anglo Canadian Gold Estates, Limited, and becoming General Manager of its operations in Rat Portage, Ontario, in 1900 Alan Sullivan changed his life in another direction as well. At the age of thirty-two he married; the courtship was a whirlwind affair. He met Bessie Salsbury Hees, daughter of Mr. and Mrs. George Hees of 174 George Street, Toronto, on February 19, 1900. On March 7 they were engaged and on December 12 they were married. In addition to the speed of the courtship, Alan's father-in-law also acted without delay. He did not want his daughter to begin her married life in Rat Portage in an unsuitable house; so between the time of the engagement and the marriage he bought property in Rat Portage and had a handsome house built for the young couple, as a wedding present. Frequent letters passed between the groom and the Hees family about the progress of the new home, which Mrs. Hees would not allow Bessie to see until she was a bride.

Bessie had been born in Oswego, New York, where she was early exposed to rich families who travelled to Europe and returned laden with antiques and art treasures. Early in life she developed difficulty with one knee, which led to surgery as early as the age of five. Later she was to have the joint removed and be left with a permanently stiff leg. This did not prevent her participation in social events, but it kept her from being athletic. The Hees family were of Dutch origin, and her mother's family English. George Hees began with a window blind factory in Oswego, and when he expanded his business to Canada he moved his family to Toronto. After her early education in Toronto at Miss Neville's School, Bessie was sent to a "finishing school" in New York, The Comstock, in Briant Square, where the New York Public Library now stands. During this period of her life Bessie was introduced to the society of house and yachting parties, balls, Newport, Saratoga, and large wardrobes of elaborate dresses. Early pictures of Bessie show her to have been extremely beautiful, with large, brown eyes and a wasp-like waist. She appeared to be petite and fragile. She frequently travelled with other members of her family and very early in life developed an absorbing interest in travel and society. When she was eighteen, she was taken on the "grand tour" of Europe by her parents.

The young couple met at the home of Mrs. Denison, the social editor of a Toronto paper. It is clear that neither family was really very happy about the marriage. Mrs. Edward Sullivan, living in genteel poverty at Sussex Court in Toronto, did not wish her son to marry into "trade," and the wealthy Hees family did not wish their daughter to marry a bearded prospector. However, the marriage took place, and it was the social event of the year in Toronto. The marriage ceremony was performed in St. James Cathedral by the Lord Bishop of Niagara and the groom's uncle, the Reverend Canon Renaud of Montreal. It was followed by a lavish reception at the Hees home, which was described by the press as a "bower of flowers." In the Bride's Book the list of gifts is impressive; from her father there was a house and lot in Rat Portage and a substantial cheque, and from her mother a sealskin coat and muff. There were many gifts of sterling silver, and from the Anglo-Canadian Mining Company a complete set of silver. One of Alan's gifts to his bride was to name the Elizabeth Gold Mine after her. The house at Rat Portage had panelled walls and was looked after by two servants: Bryant, a cockney man-servant, and Martha, a coloured maid. A second maid was added when the first child was about to arrive. On September 14, 1941, Alan Sullivan received a letter from Kenora stating that "the house you built looks fine and is lived in by a local barrister."[1] It is still in good condition and occupied. Perhaps one of the best ways to place this marriage in its proper perspective is to read the eulogy given by the Sullivans' son, Barry, at Bessie's cremation service seventy-four years later. Bessie Hees Sullivan died just before her one-hundredth birthday, at her home, 33 Eaton Square, London, England.

BESSIE SULLIVAN
1874-1974
An address at her Cremation Service
Golder's Green, March 20th.

We are gathered to say farewell to Mama, Grandmama, Great Grandmama—and in some cases to an old friend—and I hope these few words may be appropriate. In this farewell we are giving thanks for her long life. We are also losing contact with a vanished age.

Mama was probably the oldest person any of us have known, or are likely to know. Twenty six of her years belonged in the reign of Queen Victoria. She liked to tell how as a teenager she sat in a pew behind William Gladstone in Hawarden Church and heard him read the lesson; how Mark Twain, wearing a white suit, bowed

---

1 Evelyn Gienier, letter to Alan Sullivan, September 14, 1941 (in the author's files).

to her in a New York street; and the great Chinese statesman and moderniser Li Hung-Chang when staying at a Washington hotel requested that she be presented to him. She always needed to feel in touch with the life around her. In the last months of her life she was still asking: "what's the news?".

Everyone agrees she was a most remarkable old lady, the amazement of nurses, the enigma of doctors whom she threatened to survive. As a young woman she must have been unusual too— with her huge brown eyes, slight limp, and eagerness for life. What was it that made Bessie Hees with her affluent, conventional American-Canadian background, and expensive, inadequate schooling, so different from her many brothers and sisters—so different that she fell in love with, and won the devoted love of, a bearded engineer and poet, and began her married life in a log-cabin [sic] in the Canadian wilderness? What made her speak not American, but English-English when she was a girl? What made her transport her whole family to Europe in 1920, regardless of the turmoil caused—refugees, as it were, from the then cultural desert of a Canadian city?

She was, I suppose, a great romantic and not only in her imagination. She had the energy, and the money, to make many of the things she dreamed of take place. She poured her romantic feelings and aspirations chiefly, of course, into her family, into everything they did or tried to do. She made everyone aware of her intense family pride. At times it could be rather too much to be the object of that pride, but let us honour her for the embracing power of her affection. Mama always liked to believe the best of people. Anyone who married into, or became closely connected with the family, was endowed with the qualities she believed the family possessed. Let us too remember her homemaking capacity, her sparkling gaiety as a hostess, her love of giving and receiving presents (and especially flowers), her insatiable zest for travel and for people.

Why did she live so long? Was it just her great vitality, her curiosity, that kept her alive—the visits of her family, and the devoted care in her last years of three people in particular? I personally believe there was something more than this; that in those three years when she was lying bed-ridden, more and more deaf and alone, less and less able to communicate, she was going through a very private inner experience which she needed in order to balance out her life. This is a mysterious region one cannot easily speak of.

Many of us will believe that our love can reach her now, that her soul is aware of us all gathered here to pay her homage. The flowers on her coffin are a symbol of what is no longer inside. At the end of this service Michael will read a poem on immortality by her husband, Alan, that dear man whose memory we greatly treasure. It must have been written around 1897, and refers to the "short hour" of one he had much loved. In eternity even a life of ninety-nine years is brief.[2]

This eulogy reveals much about Bessie Sullivan. Despite the fact that Barry at one point lapses into poetic licence in saying his mother began her married life in a log cabin, he has captured an impression of his mother which throws light, not just on her old age, but also on her as a young bride. Although Barry believes that his father was romantic in his writing—a point open to debate—it is doubtless true that Bessie was the archetypal romantic, but, one is inclined to think, a romantic with a will of iron.

The reference to the log cabin was not a serious mistake; within two years of her marriage Bessie and Alan were living in a log cabin at the site of the Elizabeth Mine. Just before she died Bessie spoke about the log cabin—the mosquitoes, two handmade rocking chairs, and the cooking skills of Bryant, the man-servant. Despite the fact that she lived in a log cabin, Mrs. Alan Sullivan did not learn to cook and obviously never had to. Although she travelled by caboose on the Canadian Pacific and then by canoe and portage to her new home, apparently she never lowered her standard of living and continued to wear elegant clothes. She returned to Toronto in the summer of 1902, where her first child, Kathleen, was born in August at the Hees home.

Although Alan Sullivan appeared to be happily married and quite successful in his new business ventures, there were suggestions as early as 1901, and perhaps even before, that all was not as it should have been. When I searched the title to his house in the Registry Office at Kenora, I found that shortly after their marriage Sullivan had registered a lien against the house, given to his bride as a wedding present. A few years later it was sold. On the other hand, by 1903 the Anglo-Canadian Gold Estates had seven gold mining claims under development. The Elizabeth Mine, which was personally managed by Sullivan, had two shafts in operation, and the crushing of ore had begun. Many years later Sullivan

2 Barry Sullivan, address at cremation service for Bessie Sullivan, March 20, 1974 (in the author's files).

published an article with the title "Fire," which is believed to have been based on an actual incident at the Elizabeth Mine. Parts of that article follow:

It happened in Canada a good many years ago. The mine—it was a good mine, and we called it "The Elizabeth" after my wife—was on rising ground, perhaps a hundred feet above the nearest lake and half a mile from it. With the head gear as lookout point, one could see a long way in every direction, the country being broken, but without any very high elevations. It was all densely wooded. Lakes were there of every size and shape, and many a winding river with tumbling rapids, but one could not spot them from the mine—we were not high enough.

One hundred miles to the south-east stretched Lake Superior. At the same distance from the mine ran the Trans-Continental line of the C.P.R.; elsewhere one might walk two thousand miles to the Pacific and encounter hardly a soul on the way. Our part of the country was but sparsely populated with a few villages scattered along the lakes and the rivers—mere clusters of wooden houses—a few trading-posts, and some Indian encampments, which were constantly on the move. Here and there a squatter, hewing a farm out of the solid bush. That was about all. In those days we had no wireless. Communication in the summer was by canoe portage, and in winter by snowshoe and by sledge. So it was all a very stark and isolated sort of life, in which men depended entirely on their own efforts. And it was no place for the weakling in body or spirit.

At the mine we had our own independent community living in log houses. The main dwelling-camp was at the lake-side, and up at the shaft mouth we had built the usual equipment of engines, boiler rooms, hoisting gear, compressor house, etc. The water was drawn from a nearby creek, and also from underground. Our explosives were in a heavily-constructed magazine close under the lip of a low cliff, perhaps two hundred yards from the shaft. Around this spot of activity we had cleared away the bush, and created practically bare ground for an area of about an eighth of a mile in every direction from the shaft. This as a protection against possible fire.

The summer of which I write had been very hot. . . .Stringent rules were in force against fire—the greatest menace in the Canadian North—a danger doubly so because prospectors in search of mineral outcrops were only too apt to burn the moss that covered the rocky ridges. . . .

One morning in August I caught the faintest whiff of the smell that makes a man think hard in the woods—the smell of smoke! There was, as yet, no wind, but in the east the sky looked opaque, and the odour, still faint, though oddly sharp and penetrating, became more noticeable. Murdock, the mine foreman, caught it too, and we glanced at each other, a question in our eyes. Where was the fire?

At noon we knew. The air became less clear, and in the distance—it must have been forty miles away—there began to appear a large cloud of grey. This spread from north to south, moving slowly higher till it reached nearly to the zenith. No doubt of the thing now. But would it ever reach us! . . .

That night breathing was a discomfort. We lay gasping, while I realized that I had to decide something quickly. It promised to be a big fire. There was no sleep for most of us, and in the small hours I consulted with Murdock. We decided to take a chance—and fight! . . .

At mid-forenoon the visibility was low, the smoke denser, and the air more acrid. I thought anxiously of the five tons of dynamite stored in the magazine. It was packed in cases of fifty pounds each, that is fifty sticks in yellow grease paper, one and a quarter inches in diameter and about one foot long. Enough to blow St. Paul's to smithereens!

It was now evident that the fire had large proportions. On the far horizon one could see tiny forks of flame flickering up and spurting into the smoke. . . .

Then slowly, the pumps sucked dry. The mine had never been a really wet one, and we were using water faster than the workings produced it. We were left, twenty of us, without water, and half a mile from the lake, confronted by the biggest bush fire I had ever seen.

There is a point at which danger seems to create the necessary quality with which to meet it, and it does not appear that "courage" is exactly the right word for expressing that quality. At any rate, none of us thought that the others were in the least courageous. Looking back at it now, I see that what we experienced was a sort of acceptance of the inevitable. Just that. We had not done very much, though all we could, and certainly no acts of bravery had been performed. We felt decidedly sick about the affair because having all worked together in the heat, cold and discomfort to create this little hive of industry in the heart of the winderness, we considered it a d----d shame that it should be wiped out in this fashion. It was a waste which it would take months to make good. The air-compressor, boilers, hoist, all the machinery had been brought in over the ice and by a road chopped through the bush. We had built our own saw mill. Camps were made with an axe and infinite skill. Now it all seemed doomed. As to personal loss, well, the possessions of a man who lives in the woods do not amount to much . . . .

The forces of Nature were in such gigantic revolt that for a time we forgot all else, and dallied there, twenty men opposite the middle of a wall of fire forty feet high and five miles long, advancing towards us at perhaps five miles an hour. The frenzied procession of animals had ceased, the last member of it that I saw being a black bear, limping along, his head scorched, his mouth open, his small red tongue lolling loosely. What might remain behind was incinerated.

I wondered how long it would take the heavy roof of the magazine to burn through. Some time, I thought the timber being so solid. When that did go up the earth would shake, and the eruption of plunging rock and timber be scattered like deadly rain a quarter of a mile round. But by then we should be out on the lake. I got word from a panting man, just up from the sleeping camp, that all was done there that could be done. Two flat boats awaited the crew from the mine. While he spoke a burning branch alighted on the boiler-room roof. The roof began to smoke.

It was then, in that moment, that the thing happened. Now it seems like a miracle. Then it didn't.

The wind decreased, dropped and died. At one instant the hot blast was scorching our faces. In another the low savage roar was nearly obliterated. There was still noise—that of crackling timber at the edge of our clearing—but it lacked its former harsh menace. . . .[3]

This article reveals the true interest Alan Sullivan had in the struggle of man against the primeval terrain; it also shows the tremendous admiration he had for men who could stand the test when it came. We also see Sullivan's detailed knowledge of the life and work in which he was involved—exploration and mining in the Canadian wilderness. It is this side of Alan Sullivan which gave him the experience he needed as a writer.

Sullivan's experiences as a prospector for gold in the Rainy River and Lake of the Woods area were to be reflected much later in his novel *Cariboo Road*. This was a pattern he followed in much of his writing; he used his own experiences and knowledge about a certain activity in one period of time as a basis for a fictitious

3   Alan Sullivan, "Fire," *Manchester Guardian Weekly* (February 22, 1931), p. 18.

account of a similar activity in an earlier period. His experiences with the Hudson's Bay Company north of Lake Superior made possible the realism of his novel *The Fur Masters*, just as his experience with the Canadian Pacific Railway in the 1890s in northern Ontario helped him envision the story he told in *The Great Divide* of the completion of the railway through the Rockies at an earlier date. It is no coincidence that Sullivan's best writing occurs when this relationship exists between his own experiences and those of his fictional characters.

The search for gold in the Rainy River area in northwestern Ontario had begun thirty years before Sullivan discovered the Elizabeth Mine. Much excitement had accompanied this gold rush, just as it had in the gold rush on the West Coast. Development of mines in the area was slow because the railway had not yet been completed and transportation was difficult. By Sullivan's time, however, transportation was much improved, and in 1902 a ten-stamp mill was installed at the Elizabeth Mine, and 20,000 tons of ore were blocked out, but the mill operated for only a short time. This was the pattern with a large number of mines which had been opened up in the area. Most of them operated for only a few years at the beginning of the century and then closed until the 1930s, when some of them became viable mining operations. During the intervening period there were many examples of crumbling buildings and mine shafts scattered through the bush. Apparently, few of them were able to produce enough bullion to warrant continued operation. But the gold rush atmosphere existed in the area for at least ten years. Mine Centre, for example, was a boom town, with a saloon and a jail, and peopled with sharp promoters and prospectors. Some of the names of the mines suggest the atmosphere: "Money Maker," "Sugar Loaf," "The Hibernian," "Golden Crescent," "Golden Winner," and so forth. After the rush ended, the Mine Centre Hotel was dismantled into sections and moved by barge to Fort Francis, where it still stands, now named the Irwin Hotel.

Sullivan later wrote about this period of his life in his story "The Manitou Mail," in *The Passing of Oul-I-But and Other Tales*:

> If you take a pair of compasses and drop one leg into the northern end of Little Manitou Lake, and swing the other in a hundred and twenty mile circle, the curve will strike the Morning Star Mine, at least, it would a few years ago. Today it will still strike the

Morning Star—but the water is clucking contemptuously at the shaft mouth, and the grass has spread over a deserted dump. But when Strong started south on the twentieth day of one April, to be exact, he wondered if it were a glorified mint that waited him at the other side of the long stretch of rotten ice.

A small syndicate, of odorous reputation, was in control of the Star; and, strange to relate, dividends, large and lusty, were being regularly paid.[4]

When the Elizabeth Mine was forced to close, Sullivan left his position with the Anglo-Canadian Gold Estates. By 1904, he, his wife, and their daughter were living in Toronto in the St. George Apartments, and shortly after they moved to a small house on Prince Arthur Street, following the birth of D'Arcy on May 9, 1905. The third child, Natalie, was born in April, 1907. In 1908, at the age of forty, Sullivan, with his wife and three children, moved into a home bought for him by Mr. Hees, at 10 Madison Avenue, Toronto. In addition to the family, the household included a governess, a nurse, and two maids. Alan was Mechanical Superintendent of the Gutta Percha and Rubber Manufacturing Company. This must have been a very prosperous period in the life of the young family, because in 1910 all of them went on a trip to Europe, following the death of Bessie's mother, Mrs. Hees.

Kathleen, Lady Liddell Hart, who was about eight years old at that time, has vivid recollections of what life was like on Madison Avenue. She speaks of her father as having a dressing room with a desk where at weekends he wrote short stories and verse, and writers and publishers came to the house and Mrs. Sullivan had Sunday morning breakfast parties for professors and authors. Kidney and bacon in a rich sauce was served from a chafing dish and rolls and coffee. For many years her image of a professor was that of Professor George Mavor who had a magnificent beard and looked like an Old Testament prophet. The children were not present at these breakfasts as they all had their meals in the schoolroom except lunch on Sundays.[5]

Alan Sullivan refers to this same period in a passage quoted earlier about his need to write in order to keep a balance between

---

4   Alan Sullivan, *The Passing of Oul-I-But and Other Tales* (Toronto: J. M. Dent, 1913), p. 107.

5   Lady Liddell Hart, notes about her father entitled "Some Memories of my father, Alan Sullivan" (1976; copy in the author's files).

the technical side of his brain and the imaginative one. Sullivan had been publishing short stories and verse since 1893, and his first book was published in 1912. *I Believe That* _____ , incorrectly described in most bibliographies as a book of essays, is a book of aphorisms. These short, pithy statements by Sullivan are sometimes amusing, sometimes cynical, and sometimes profound; they foreshadow many of the themes he is later to develop more fully in his fiction. A few examples follow:

> A Woman's glance, like a lighthouse, often illuminates a dangerous course.[6]

> The talkative person is criticized for every indiscretion, but the silent one is credited with many a profundity he could never have uttered.[7]

> Only an unintelligent man will say that he understands a woman.[8]

In 1913 the family moved to a new home, designed and built by Sullivan himself, in Wychwood Park in Toronto. Lady Liddell Hart has written of life in this new home:

> When we moved to the house father designed in Wychwood Park he had a proper study on the third floor on the north west corner. The house was very modern with a flat roof, an engineer's house and much criticised at the time. The study had a large desk, a comfortable sofa and a large fireplace. It smelt pungently of wood smoke. Father was the most unpossessive man I have ever known and shared everything even letting his study be used in the winter months by six friends of mine who met weekly to talk and cook extraordinary messes over the fire. Father's hospitality and humour are well remembered by the surviving members of that group today in Toronto.
>
> To be taken camping by father is one of my happiest memories. First we had to learn to paddle a canoe kneeling in Indian fashion, and how to right one if overturned. He showed us how to make beds of spruce branches and with many layers so one could almost bounce up and down they were so springy. He baked bannock in the wood fire ashes, and the thick bacon in the pan frying with the eggs smelt delicious. To end the day there was a story about Indians he had known.

---

6 Alan Sullivan, *I Believe that* _____ (Toronto: Wm. Tyrrell and Co., 1912), p. 1.
7 Ibid., p. 51.
8 Ibid.

One winter when the snow was exceptionally deep and the pond in Wychwood Park deeply frozen and ideal for skating, father with the help of the older children built three communicating igloos from blocks of hard snow cut in Eskimo fashion. I have a photograph of the family and the Hees cousins sitting outside them and the group includes George who must have been about six years old. The igloos lasted for many weeks and were a perfect shelter from icy winds when we changed our skates.[9]

When Alan Sullivan moved from the Elizabeth Mine to Toronto, his life changed completely. In all probability his position at Gutta Percha was obtained with the assistance of his influential father-in-law, George Hees, who was a director of several companies and was extremely well-known in Toronto's social and business circles. But Alan's duties during those years as Mechanical Superintendent of Gutta Percha were, as described earlier, "confined, arduous, exacting and mechanical." It is my opinion that he found more than his position "confining." There are many men, and Sullivan was one of them, to whom the routine of married life is cage-like. This is not to suggest that such men do not enjoy the company of women; to the contrary, they quite frequently appear to enjoy the company of several women, but usually on their own terms. In addition, Sullivan craved the outdoor life, which he had given up when he left Northern Ontario.

From 1904 until 1917 Sullivan played the role of one who was at least on the fringe of Toronto's Establishment. He and his wife took an active part in the social activities that accompanied that level of society. But it must be remembered that this was the period when "Toronto the Good" was not just a catch phrase. To a man who enjoyed the company of other men in the outdoors and life with the Indians in tents and cabins, the phrase was probably "Toronto the Boring." As he did so often in later life, Sullivan managed to escape at times from family life; for example, he played a very active role in the Toronto Arts and Letters Club, which was exclusively male. He prospected frequently during these years when he was employed in industry. But the life of concerts at Massey Hall, plays at the Royal Alexandra Theatre, and the incessant round of dinners, receptions, and "At Homes" must have been hard for him to endure.

---

9   Lady Liddell Hart, "Some Memories of my father."

He did take great pride in the magnificent house which he had designed for his family. It still has a splendid appearance among the Elms of Wychwood Park and would have provided the perfect setting for a family near the top of the Toronto social ladder. But it would always be only near the top, because with the fabulous fortunes and social positions of the Eatons, the Masseys, the Mulocks, the Flavelles, and so forth, the Alan Sullivan family was to remain on the fringe of that exclusive circle. This fact possibly did not affect Alan very much, but Bessie Sullivan did not enjoy the type of Toronto life to which she was exposed. By now she must have realized that Alan was a man who would not continue in a career in industry or business and that eventually she was going to have to depend on the wealth of the Hees family for financial security. His other ambition, that of being a successful writer, did not interest her greatly. In addition, there may have been some gossip about her husband. He was exceedingly handsome and had great appeal to women. When I first started this study I received a series of mysterious long distance phone calls from a man who at first would not identify himself. He claimed to have one-hundred and five love letters written by Sullivan to his mother between the years 1901 and 1914. Eventually, he gave me the name of the woman who was the recipient of those letters and offered to turn the letters over to me as long as I would not reveal the identity of his mother. I became sceptical of the whole project as the negotiations proceeded and decided that it was a hoax. It suggested to me, however, that such rumours may have attended Sullivan in his lifetime as well.

3

During this period in Toronto a major event occurred in Sullivan's life: in 1913 his first book of fiction was published. *The Passing of Oul-I-But and Other Tales* is a collection of sixteen short stories, some of which had been published earlier in *The Atlantic Monthly*, *Harper's Magazine*, and *Scribner's Magazine*. One story in the collection stands out as representing Sullivan's ideals and also as reflecting the interest he had retained in the life he had not experienced for over a dozen years. The story, "The Essence of a Man," tells of Tom Moore, a Metis, who is sent with a load of provisions from the Hudson Bay Post at Ignace in northern Ontario to the post at Lac Seul, a trip of 215 miles. After Tom sets out with his load of 300 pounds on a toboggan drawn by his dogs, he is assailed by two enemies: a blizzard and a lynx. The lynx succeeds in fatally wounding three of his huskies; the other two escape after stealing some of the provisions. Tom pulls the toboggan himself to its destination. The story is one of courage, loyalty, determination, and an absolute standard of integrity; it also exemplifies Sullivan's ability to capture the atmosphere of northern life with a sharply realistic pen.

Through level lines of streaming snow, a huge figure loomed large and portentous. Vanishing in blinding gusts, it ever and ever appeared again, thrusting itself onward with dogged persistence. Across flat and frozen plains forged the great piston-like legs driving down his snowshoes with a clocklike regularity that suggested, rather than told of, enormous muscular force. Beyond him, knee-deep, toiled five yellow coated black-muzzled dogs, their shoulders jammed tight into their collars, their tawny sides rippling with the play of straining tendons; and last of all, a long, low toboggan lurched indomitably on, the trampled trail breaking into a surge of powdered snow under its curving bow. Into the teeth of the gale pushed this pigmy caravan—a gale that was born on the flat shores of Hudson Bay, that breasted the slopes of the Height of Land, that raged across the blank white expanse of Lac Seul, and was now shrieking down, dire and desolate, to the icebound and battlemented border of Lake Superior. It was a wind that had weight. Tom Moore felt its vast and impalpable force, as he leaned against it, when he stopped for breath. It assaulted him—it smoothed out the crumpled trail as the wake of a ship is obliterated by closing waters—till, a moment after his passing, the snow ridges lay trackless and unruffled. Still, however insignificant in these formless wastes, that silent progress held steadily on; and so it had from early morn. . . .

. . . .

Long ago, when his mother died, she had warned him against the false new gods which the white man had brought from the big sea water, and in her old faith had turned her face to the wall of her teepee. She had been buried in a tree top, near a bend of the Albany River, where it turns north from Nipigon and runs through the spruce forests that slope down to Hudson's Bay. But Tom had listened to the new story—more than that, he had hewed square timber for the Mission Church at Ignace; and now retribution had come, at last. No sooner had the idea formulated itself, than it seized upon him; and then there rose to meet it—defiance.

Grimly, he slackened the collar from the dead husky, and laid the empty traces across his own breast; savagely he thrust forward, and started the toboggan, and the diminished company stayed and stopped not till, once again, the darkness came.

. . . .

Drunkenly and unseeingly, but with blind, indomitable purpose, the man won every agonizing step. His snowshoes were smashed to a shapeless tangle of wood and sinew; his face was gaunt, patched with grey blots of frost-bite; and through his sunken cheeks, the high bones stood out like knuckles on a clenched fist. Ice was plastered on his cap and lay fringed on brow and lids, but beneath them burned eyes that glowed with dull fires, quenchless and abysmal. By infinitesimal degrees he drew in, with not a wave of the hand, not a sign of recognition. Up the path from shore, to trading post, shouldered the titan figure, till it reached the door. At the latch, stiff, frozen fingers were fumbling, as Anderson flung it open; and then a vast bulk darkened the threshold, swung in helpless hesitation for a fraction of time, and pitched, face foremost, on the rough pine floor. . . .

"No eat for five days' pull toboggan. No dogs."

Anderson stiffened where he sat. "What's that? Haulin' three hunder' of grub, and ye were starving? Ye big copper-coloured fule!"

"No packer's grub, boss; Hudson Bay grub!"

It was almost a groan, for Tom was far spent.

Involuntarily the quiet Scot lifted his hands in amazement, and then hurried into his kitchen, murmuring, as he disappeared: "Man, man, it's with the likes of ye that the Hudson Bay keeps its word."[10]

This story, published in 1913, indicates that Sullivan was much ahead of his time in his understanding of the native peoples of Canada and of the north of Canada. In a letter, Barry Sullivan has written the following:

I imagine that my father through his direct contact with the Indian peoples must have recorded visually and empathetically some vanished aspect of their life. Where his sympathies lay is beyond doubt. . . . I am on the track of a letter which father wrote to *The Times* in, I think 1937, in which he spoke of the failure of the Canadian Government to realize its responsibilities for the Indian

---

10   Alan Sullivan, "The Essence of a Man," in *The Passing of Oul-I-But and Other Tales* (Toronto: Dent, 1913), pp. 49-64.

and Eskimo population of the north; it was also a moving plea far ahead of its time for ecological awareness.[11]

The other fifteen stories in this volume are mostly about Indian experience and attitudes. Against a background of snow, wind, and frequent darkness, each tale suggests a characteristic of Indian life and, in a sense, of man. "The Passing of Oul-i-but" expresses "the mystical shadow of mortality" and the Indian stoical acceptance of death. The resiliency of man and his ability to survive is stressed. Other stories tell of a Royal Canadian Mounted Police officer who dies protecting his patrol, of justifiable revenge, of loyalty to duty, and of the essential beauty of the stark wilderness. Despite civilization, modern man and primeval man are seen to share the same essential qualities. The stories reflect, in their accuracy of detail and atmosphere, the personal experience of Sullivan.

Sullivan was now turning away from his interest in engineering and industry toward writing. In 1913 he wrote an article "John A. Pearson, Master Builder" for *The Yearbook of Canadian Art*, a publication of The Toronto Arts and Letters Club; he served as President of the club in 1914-15. Eventually, he gave up his position at Gutta Percha to devote all his time to writing. In 1914 *Blantyre—Alien* was published. Set in Yorkton, obviously Toronto, the story is about Dr. Brian Blantyre and Stella Blake, and the link between them, a doctor named Stephen Ellison. Brian had met Stella while he was a ship's doctor and she was a passenger on the ship. After they marry and settle in Yorkton, he realizes that he does not belong—he is an alien. When Stella begins work with Stephen on a committee concerned with the setting up of homes for victims of tuberculosis, her marriage to Brian begins to collapse. Blantyre leaves his lucrative practice to work in the slums, where he is able to be a person who stands out against his surroundings. He then returns to the sea and is involved in a shipwreck, at which time his natural heroism emerges. He commits suicide at the end of the book in order to leave Stella free. Sullivan weaves into this tragic romantic narrative a comprehensive picture of Canadian life, including the political situation: the end of the Laurier era, an era which is treated as a national awakening. He also depicts the Canadian identity:

---

11   Barry Sullivan, letter to Gordon D. McLeod, October 12, 1975.

On the ship were many English travellers, but more Canadian. Blantyre, now from the inside, studied them with interest. Of the English people some were going to live in Canada. Its virile prosperity was a magnet. It drew them away from a life of fruitless effort, arduous and unproductive, whose object was the difficult maintenance of social position, whose future was nebulous and unpromising. In spite of blood and breeding, in spite of custom and tradition and countless memories, there was now no room for them at home. Blantyre knew what it meant. He felt something of what they felt.

The others interested him most—returning to all corners of Canada, confident people who accepted cheerfully all Britain and the Continent had to offer, then set their faces westward on the long trail home. Lawyers, brokers, manufacturers, all seemed to enjoy life with an unhesitating acceptance of the future. Blantyre was struck by the freedom of their thoughts. What would have been business confidences in England were here discussed without reserve. There was none of that English reticence, that coldness which is, after all, merely an unwillingness to appear too interested in other people's affairs. They were interested, and said so frankly.

They were patriotic, these Canadians. They loved that element of English life which understood their own country. They spoke quizzically of British formalities, but with the affection of a boy for his school. He could see that they were divided between respect for British traditions and unwillingness to hitch their own waggons to any individual star, however ancient and glorious.[12]

This passage reveals Sullivan's understanding of a major dichotomy in Canadian life: the tension between the influence of the British past and the desire for freedom from any such past—the dream of an independent Canada.

4

During the early part of World War I Alan Sullivan had completely shed his engineering role; he was referred to in the press as the "Toronto poet and author," and his works of fiction were the subject of many reviews by well-known critics in the magazines and newspapers of the time. This was just the beginning of such press coverage; although Sullivan was never the subject of a scholarly article in an academic journal, as his novels appeared they received a tremendous number of reviews, throughout the

---

12   Alan Sullivan, *Blantyre—Alien* (London: J. M. Dent, 1914), pp. 48-49.

English-speaking world. He was enjoying his life as a writer, and his family life in Wychwood Park was also happy. Natalie, Madame Coulet, still speaks of the trips on which he took the children to Chief's Island on Lake Joseph in Muskoka, where they joined with the Ketchum family in fishing, canoeing, and other outdoor activities. The Ketchum "boys," who later became leaders in Canadian educational circles, stayed at the same summer boarding house in Port Hope as the Sullivan children, who were sent there with a governess each summer. A surprise development in the Sullivan family was the arrival of, first, one baby brother, Barry, in 1915, and a second, Michael, in 1916, when their father was forty-seven and forty-eight respectively. Apparently, Grandfather Hees was more than surprised; he resented the fact that his daughter was having these two young boys to look after and did not include them in the provisions he made in his will for his other grandchildren, or perhaps he neglected to change his will.

In 1917 *The Inner Door* was published. It is based on Sullivan's experiences at Gutta Percha; the plot concerns the Consumer Rubber Company, which had been willed by the founder, James Percival, to his daughter Sylvia, who is engaged to be married to Kenneth Landon. The Landon family lose their money, and while Sylvia is living in Mentone in France, Kenneth becomes a labourer in the factory under an assumed name. The theme concerns the conflict between management and labour in the early part of this century; that conflict becomes polarized around the positions taken by the two lovers. Landon appears to receive a regenerative effect from honest work and eventually marries the daughter of the labour leader in the factory and replaces that leader when the latter is accidentally killed during a labour dispute. The title refers to doors being opened in the mind of Landon. Sullivan's personal sympathies are clearly with labour in this novel, despite the fact that his social life in Toronto at the time was exclusively with members of the industrial and financial establishment.

In the same year, when he was forty-nine, Sullivan enlisted in the Royal Air Force. Although he learned to fly a plane, he was refused a licence as a pilot because of his age. Ironically, he once had to take over the controls of a plane to save it from crashing. He was involved in one crash landing in Canada on August 11, 1917. The newspaper account follows:

AIRPLANE CRASH
AT PORT HOPE

Lieut. Alan Sullivan of Toronto
and Capt. W. Eastwood, Peterboro,
in Charge

Port Hope, Aug. 11.—Capt. W. Eastwood and Lieut. Alan Sullivan of the Leaside, Toronto, camp of the R.A.F. visited town to-day in their machine, No. C215, and made a landing on the Trinity College school grounds. About two o-clock they left, intending to go to Cobourg, but in rising the engine failed to operate properly, and they struck the trees at the town park and the machine crashed to the ground. Lieut. Sullivan received a rather severe scalp wound, and was removed to the Port Hope Hospital. Capt. Eastwood escaped injury. The machine is a total wreck.

Capt. Eastwood is a son of Dr. Eastwood of Peterboro, and left here with the 39th. Battalion, transferring to the Flying Corps upon reaching England. He was wounded and invalided home several months ago.

It is expected that Lieut. Sullivan will be able to leave the hospital tomorrow. He is the well-known Toronto poet and novelist.[13]

His experiences in the Royal Air Force and with the fledgling aircraft industry in Canada prepared Sullivan to write *Aviation in Canada: 1917-1918*, which was published in 1919. It should be noted that in the front of that volume the following item is printed: "While the contents of this volume present an accurate history of the R.A.F. Canada, it is to be understood that the Air Ministry is not responsible for any statements made herein." This notice places Sullivan in the position of having been the unofficial historian of the R.A.F. Canada. The book covers, in considerable technical detail, the organization and operation of this branch of the Canadian Armed Services, in the last years of World War I. Sullivan held the rank of Lieutenant in the Royal Engineer's Section of the R.A.F. I have received a letter from Havelock C. Graham, who was a young Acting Flight Commander, "A" Flight in the 88th Squadron, R.A.F., stationed at Camp Borden in the summer of 1918. He writes:

---

13 *The Mail and Empire*, Toronto, August 12, 1917.

On several occasions I had the privilege and pleasure of ferrying Mr. Sullivan who was a "brass hat" Staff Officer between Armour Heights Airdrome, Toronto and Camp Borden. Just what Mr. Sullivan's actual rank was escapes me but I know I was very impressed by the gold braid on the peak of his cap.

Just why I was chosen for this duty I do not know but I do remember it as an enjoyable one. Mr. Sullivan was not a pilot but when we got into the air I would ask him over the crude intercom that we had in the old Curtiss JN4 machines if he would like to take over and he always expressed his pleasure at my invitation.

We would also converse during the short flights about literature and books and he gave me a copy of one of his novels. . . . I remember him as a gentleman and a scholar who made a lasting impression on a youth who had just completed one year in Engineering at the University.[14]

Little did the young pilot know that Alan Sullivan had also completed only one year in engineering at the University.

After the war, Sullivan remained in Toronto, where he continued to write, but he also returned to his work as an explorer and prospector. At some point in time, either during these few years or perhaps earlier, when he was involved in a mining operation at Cobalt, he had mined enough silver to be made into a silver bar which he treasured as a momento of his mining days. It was one of the few material possessions he wished to keep. The bar was in a vault in Toronto. Unfortunately, without consulting her husband about it, Bessie Sullivan is alleged to have disposed of the bar.

The Rapids, mentioned earlier, in Chapter II, was published in 1920 but had been written considerably before that date. It is reasonable to assume that the impression Clergue had made on the young Sullivan remained with him throughout his life. Sullivan's mining ventures, his attempts at being an inventor, and probably even his years in industry were all part of his search for wealth. The connection between Clergue and Sullivan in this respect is obvious: Clergue, the entrepreneur, represented to Sullivan one ideal which he followed quite separately from the part of him that was the writer. *The Rapids*, in addition to painting an accurate portrait of Clergue as a man of vision tinged with tragedy, contains a romantic story linking Clergue with Elsie Worden, which also ends on a tragic note. The book received favourable reviews and was success-

---

14   Havelock D. Graham, letter to Gordon D. McLeod, May 3, 1975.

ful both as a book and a film—which Sullivan never saw. This novel, or perhaps the one that followed it, marks the end of Sullivan's life in Canada for a time, because later in 1920 he was to move abruptly to England.

IV

The European Years

1

In June of 1920 Alan Sullivan, prospecting in Alaska, received a telegram from his wife, which read: "Have booked passage entire family England." This decision was made possible by the death of her father, which left her a considerable share of his estate. Kathleen, Lady Liddell Hart, who was eighteen at the time, remembers the confusion and consternation that resulted. Her mother had the ability to make the decisions connected with moving and travelling, but always became unwell during the packing and moving arrangements. Kathleen and D'Arcy, with assistance from the Renaud relatives, made all the arrangements for storing the contents of the large house and packing the necessary clothing for the whole family. Unfortunately, no clearly laid plans were ever made for a home on the other side of the Atlantic, and following the uprooting of the family from Toronto there were six years of constant moving and travelling. The disruption in the education of Kathleen and D'Arcy was more serious than in the case of Natalie; the two young boys were not yet of school age. It was at this time that Kathleen took on the responsibility of being second mother to her two young brothers; this responsibility remained hers until they were old enough to look after themselves. The move and its effect on the family have been discussed earlier; the decision itself was never explained by Bessie.

One can only conclude that Bessie was bored with the prospect of life in Toronto and yearned for the more romantic life of travel and European society. She certainly never lost her taste for it. Although there were beneficial effects for at least some of the children, the benefits, if any, to her husband will always be open to question. It is possibly true that had Sullivan remained in Canada he might never have received genuine recognition, as he did in England and, eventually, in America. Perhaps, like Morley Callaghan, it was necessary that he be an exile before Canada would grant him any real recognition. Even after twenty years exile the recognition was meagre. He was awarded a Governor General's Award when he was seventy-five years of age, but his name soon dropped from sight in the Canadian literary scene. Perhaps he would never have achieved the success that he did with his novel *The Great Divide*, and it might never have been filmed as *The Great Barrier*, had he not lived in England, where he rubbed shoulders with writers, publishers, and film producers. Sullivan, in 1929, wrote in retrospect about the move and its effect on his writing:

> I discovered at once that in England there is tremendous literary competition, and an unusually high percentage of people in this country write well. They are also content to write for very moderate payment. Thus, to bring oneself into English literary circles and at the same time to realize earnings sufficient to justify the attempt, was not altogether easy. But that experience is now a thing of the past, and in the last eight years I have written about twelve novels, these appearing serially first, then in book form, one semi-technical volume and perhaps seventy or eighty short stories for English, Canadian and American magazines. During this time Dent brought out my second book of short stories, "Under the Northern Lights," from which I am about to broadcast a selection of six, and the same book is being used as a school reader for purposes of instruction in literary composition. A British film company has acquired picture rights for three novels; I expect the pictures will be made this winter, so, altogether, the transition stage from Canada to England may be said to be over.[1]

In August, 1920 the Sullivan family sailed on the *Empress of France* for Britain. After landing at Liverpool, the family went to Bettws-y-Coed in Wales, a place previously visited by the smaller Sullivan family in 1910. Perhaps one of the best ways to gain insight into the type of life the Sullivans lived in Europe is to read

---

1   Alan Sullivan, "In the Matter of Alan Sullivan," *Ontario Library Review* 14 (November, 1929), 35-36.

segments from the book *And Then We Went*, written by Barry
Sullivan and privately printed by his father in 1925, when Barry
was only ten years old. It is a collection of his notes, written from
time to time, about the family. The spelling and grammar were
not edited by his father. It should be explained that the younger
boys called their father Doop and sometimes Doop'o; they also
referred to their older sister, Kathleen, by several other names.
This first little book by Barry covers the period from the arrival in
Britain in 1920 until the two younger boys were entered in a
preparatory school by their father in 1924. The beginning of the
extract that follows refers to the Sullivans' first move after their
visit to Wales:

> Then we went to Bornmouth in Dorsetshire, I soon got tired of it.
> Then we went to London where we spent Michael's birthday . . . .
>   We spent Christmas at Wyndham Place. We got a tin train
> and a bridge and some briks. (Our governess at that time was Miss
> Lucas). We stayed there five months.
>   Then we went to the South of France [1921] to St. Raphael.
> Once Doop'o made a stone house and built a fire inside it. And
> another time Doop made a bridge and a station out of stone and we
> had our tine train running, it was very great Doopish sport, After
> we left St. Raphael we gradually made our way home to England.
> We first of all went to Avignon, where we stayed at three or four
> Hotels . . . . Then we crossed over to England by Calais to Dover,
> then we went to London, we stayed at the Grosvenor Hotel. From
> the Grosvenor Hotel we went to Uckfield. . . . We did not like it
> very much, so we went to Crowborough at the Beacon Hotel. . . .
> From the Beacon Hotel we went to Isomer on the Thames. . . .
> From Isomer we went to nine Onslow Square in London, for
> Christmas. . . . Just before Christmas we had a new governess her
> name was Miss Handcock. . . . After nine Onslow Square we
> decided to go to Italy [1922] We went to Paris, and took train de
> Luxe to Naples, we stopped at Rome an hour, we arrived at Naples
> about two o'clock at night. . . . In a few days we went over to Capri
> three hours from Naples with Mummy . . . After Capri we went to
> Rome with mother, it was very hot and derty, I was very glad to get
> out of it. Then we went to Florence with Mummy. . . . Then
> Doop'o came down to Florence, it was very nice to see him.
>   After Florence we went to Milan where Doop'o bought all my
> birthday presents which was in two days. We saw the great
> Cathedral with all the spires. . . . And we saw the picture of the
> "Last Supper". On the 7th. of June 1922 which is my birthday we

went to Tremezzo on Lake Como. . . . After Tremezzo we went to Rapallo, we only stayed there one night and the next day we went to the Emperial Palance at Santa Marghereta. Mini and D'Arcy and Mother went on to Florence, where they took a flat for Christmas [1923] After Florence we went to Rapallo. . . . And Mother took Mimi, D'Arcy and Mr. Henderson to Perguia. And then Mother took Mimi to a school in Florence. In the middle of April we started off for Brussels. We went to Milan, and as we got on the train for Basle Pow-Pow found she haden't her Passport so she got off the train just as it had started, and got a new passport and had it signed by an Italian Countess. . . . The next day we went to Brussels. D'oop'o came on Good Friday. . . .

After Brussels we went to Ostend with Mother and took a ship for Dover and went to Victoria where Doop'o met us. In two days we went to Downs Farm in Devonshire, . . . Mother and Doop stayed in a hotel in front of the beach, and Mimi stayed in the farm. We lived there three months.

In the end of July we went to Middle Old Park in Farnham. . . . Doop wrote The Jade God in Farnham. We stayed there ten months.

In the middle of June [1924] we went to London. We went to a day school in Sloan Squaer and we used to play cricket in Acton Town. In the middle of July Mimi and Michael and I went to St. Briac in Brittany, . . . We landed and crossed over in a vidette to Dinard and had lunch in Mrs. Costers Villa and went in a tram from Dinard to St. Briac called the Demoiselle and it was very noisy.

We lived in a fisherman's house and had all our meals out of doors. . . . Mother and Natalie and Doop came to Dinard and we joined them in about ten days. We lived in a villa with a very nice Belgian family called Von Schelles. Doop stayed in the Villa Mon Repos in the Vicomte where he was writing and I went and had lunch with him. . . .

In the end of September 1924 Doop Michael and I went to London and the crossing was very rough, and we went to bed early. Doop bought us many clothes and the tailor showed us Guliver with all the little people round him. He was made of plaster. Then we went to the Zoo to say goodbye to the animals and then the next day took us to Fonthill School, East Grinstead, Sussex.[2]

It is interesting and informative to view these four disorganized years through the eyes of a boy who at the beginning is five

2 Barry Sullivan, *And Then We Went* (privately printed, 1925), pp. 9-21.

years of age and at the end about nine. His innocent statements about Doop's arrivals and departures reveal the extent to which Sullivan isolated himself from his family, whether for the sake of his writing or because he did not enjoy the life-style. It is also interesting to note that Bessie rarely is pictured as the mother. It is usually the latest governess or Mimi (Kathleen) who performs that function. When Sullivan entered Michael and Barry at Fonthill School, he was starting them on typical British educational careers, which were to be completed at Oxford for Barry and at Cambridge for Michael, after both had completed Fonthill and then Rugby. From a modern point of view, the type of life pictured by Barry is almost unbelievable, but, even in the twenties, it was unusual for a family of five children to be moved from pillar to post without a permanent home. One gets the impression that Bessie was in her heyday. By 1923 she had established herself in English society to such an extent that she and her two daughters were presented at court. The picture of Bessie in court dress reveals her to be beautiful and still very youthful in appearance. Lady Liddell Hart explains that, to Sullivan, it was all a lot of nonsense, and during the whole procedure he merely acted as chauffeur.

During these first years in Europe, Alan was writing but at first not much publishing took place. In 1921, *Brother Eskimo*, juvenile fiction probably written while Sullivan was still in Canada, appeared. This story about "survival" tells of the testing of two young Eskimo boys deliberately left behind when the village moves. It realistically presents the natural cycle, and also a sensible attitude toward Canada's native people:

> If by chance you ever get well north of Southampton Island . . . and see the brown faced folk in their egg-shell igloos, don't be in the least sorry for them or try to get them to wear American clothes, which would not fit and in which they would freeze to death, but remember that they are just as happy as you are and probably a deal more comfortable and as proud of their ice-floe as you are of New York, or Cincinnati or Poughkeepsie.[3]

Gradually, however, Sullivan was successful in having some of his novels published in serialized form, and he was also producing short stories and articles; this was at the height of the popularity of

---

3   Alan Sullivan, *Brother Eskimo* (Toronto: McClelland and Stewart, 1921), p. 226.

magazines, and he was a very capable short story writer. It is almost impossible to discuss Sullivan's formidable output of short stories, except those published in book form. In addition, he published *The Birthmark* in 1924, followed by two more novels in 1925; of the latter, *The Crucible* was the first novel written under the pseudonym Sinclair Murray. Obviously set, for the most part, in Rat Portage in northwestern Ontario, where Sullivan himself first worked as a mining engineer, the novel begins and ends in England. The story, which involves much intrigue, too explicitly sets out characters as being either good or evil: "On one side of the bullion there now stood three persons representing all that was decent and straight and courageous. On the other were cornered those other two for whom trickery and cowardice had no refuge left."[4] There is considerable use of symbolism in this story centred in the Victrix Mine and the crucible, which was used to extract the pure gold and also, by analogy, to separate the pure people from those who were not so pure. Life in the small mining community was treated by Sullivan as a microcosm of the world: "Thus in a far corner of the forest there was being enacted in a pigmy community the ancient drama of love, desire, rivalry, and human effort."[5] Having lived himself in Rat Portage and then at the Elizabeth Mine, Sullivan was in a good position to write about such a microcosm; he does so with considerable realism.

Also published in 1925 was *The Jade God*, a mystery set in Sussex, England. This novel belongs completely to Sullivan's "English period"; it has not only an English setting but also content that one would expect from an English writer of the 1920s. Beech Lodge, which has been rented by John Derrick, a writer, contains the mystery of the murder of its original owner. Although in outward appearance the estate is paradisal, the inner atmosphere of the house, and especially the den, is quite the opposite. Fate plays a prominent role in the plot:

> These actors were only discharging their parts in an endless play that would continue with its constantly changing scenes. . . . The entire universe is throbbing and quivering with such records that he who can may read or at least perceive.[6]

4   Sinclair Murray (pseud.), *The Crucible* (London: Bles, 1925), p. 284.
5   Ibid., p. 139.
6   Alan Sullivan, *The Jade God* (Toronto: F. D. Goodchild, 1925), p. 253.

The story contains most of the elements necessary for successful, gripping mystery, in the style of Agatha Christie. Some years later, in collaboration with William Edwin Barry, the book was dramatized and had a very successful run on Broadway. At the time of Sullivan's death, he and Barry were attempting to negotiate the movie rights for the play. The book and the play were favourably reviewed by critics on both sides of the Atlantic.

The Sullivan family, with the exception of the two young boys and Kathleen, were in Europe until Christmas of 1924, when they converged on a flat in Cadogan Court, London. After Christmas and until April, Sullivan was in Portofino on the Italian Riviera, but during the summer of 1925 the family rented Barn House at Sonning-on-Thames. Granny Sullivan came from Canada to join them. There were other visitors that summer as well: boyfriends of Kathleen and Natalie, and Sir John Murray, Sullivan's publisher, among others. It was a happy family summer. In the autumn, Bessie, accompanied by Natalie, went to New York and Canada for a visit, which lasted until February of 1926.

2

On June 1, 1926, Alan and Bessie Sullivan leased Sheerland House at Pluckley, Kent. This was their first home since leaving Wychwood Park, Toronto, in August, 1920, and it was to be their home until 1940, when the house was subject to requisition by the army in the face of the expected invasion. The comfortable house with its large grounds was on the estate of Sir Henry Deering, who lived in Surrenden House. Sheerland House had an entrance hall, a drawing room, dining room, study, and washroom on the main floor with six bedrooms on the second floor, and three servants' rooms. As another sign of the new stability, Alan bought the first car the family had owned since leaving Canada. The house was surrounded by lovely farmland, and was approached by a long elm-lined drive. It appeared that the Sullivan family had finally found a home and, what was more important, a home life.

There were other signs of stability in the family, not the least of which was the engagement of Kathleen to Tim Nelson, who was to become her husband on January 22, 1927. Nelson, who developed into a brilliant surgeon, died suddenly from an operating room mishap in 1935, leaving Kathleen with two young daughters. Despite the security the home provided for the family, it did not bring an end to the travels of the family. Following the wedding of their daughter, the Sullivans spent the rest of the winter in Algiers and Tunis. Natalie attended the Sorbonne in Paris. This was typical of the years to come—but there was a home with their own furniture and possessions and a sense of belonging. Throughout the years since first leaving Canada, Sullivan had returned there many times, the first trip being as early as the autumn of 1920. He continued to be interested in several projects in Canada as well as in England which were not related to his writing. One of these was his invention, the Hydrotomaut, which was to create energy by the perpetual motion of the downward movement of water.

Whether it was a result of moving to Sheerland House or not, despite his various trips with or without Bessie, and the comings and goings of his five children and their various problems, and his various other interests, Sullivan published, in the first five years after moving into Sheerland House, no less than seventeen books.

He appeared to enjoy the life of a country gentleman, although he did not always fit the mould. He behaved properly when he delivered the Remembrance Day Address at the parish church in Pluckley, but he rebelled against a person like Sir James Dunn. Dunn, who had been linked to Sullivan's ideal, Clergue, as early as 1907, rented the large home of Sir Henry Deering for a time and decided to lock the gates leading into the long drive which the Sullivans were accustomed to using. Sullivan smashed the locks with a chisel and hammer. When Sir James came by on horseback in the role of country squire to protest, he was hailed from an upstairs window by Sullivan, who was shaving, with, "Hello Jimmy. I think I'm the man you are looking for." Dunn had not realized that Sullivan was his neighbour.

One of the more revealing accounts of Sullivan's life at Sheerland House comes from Sells, the Chauffeur-gardener-handyman, who stayed with the family during their fourteen years in the house:

> In 1926 I came to Sheerland and I stayed with the family for 14 years; then they went to Canada. I found him one of the whitest men that ever lived ... he was very direct and he would do anything for anyone. ...
>
> He had a faint trace of the Canadian accent, but it was not pronounced, but whenever he used to come back from Canada, he always used to greet me with these words: "Boodjoo, Sekanakaney." And so I asked him once what they meant and he said "that's Eskimo for a greeting to a friend."

He was a well-bred man—he was *akin* to an English gentleman by his ways and manners and the way he used to treat all men, whether rich or poor. I'll tell you what he used to think a great deal about, and take pleasure in doing, and that was he and I going down the wood and sawing down big limbs of fallen trees and then we used to saw them up in small lengths, and take them up to the house—he used to revel in that and he really could swing an axe—he really could. If he got fed up with sitting indoors writing he used to say "Come on Sells, let's go down to the wood and have a bit of exercise," and we used to clear off there. One day we were talking about the youngsters of that day, how they were all so lively and that, and he said I expect they alter when they get old, and I turned round and said to him "Youth never grows old. . . ." We had some happy times together one way and another.

He used to treat me just as though we were a couple of brothers or old cronies. I don't think that all the time I was with him we had a bad word, or an occasion for to sort of get upset over me. . . . He was always very jokey when he could be. He always used to have a joke with the head-porter of the Savage Club in London.[7]

Just as revealing is the letter that Sullivan wrote to Sells in response to a request for a letter of recommendation:

You came to us fourteen years ago, and since then we have all regarded you more as a friend and member of the family than anything else. Always you have been devoted, thoughtful and kind. Sheerland House would not have been Sheerland House without you. Never under any circumstance have you failed us always putting aside your own convenience to be of all the help you could.

You are an excellent gardener: you understand both flowers and vegetables, and considering the amount of garden of both kinds you had to look after single-handed, we think you did excellent work, and kept us always well supplied.

In addition to all this you're a first-class driver, and can keep a car in good condition; you're a bit of a plumber, and have saved us many a professional visit in that way: you're a good painter and a fair electrician. In fact you have shown yourself an unusually all round man.[8]

---

7 Transcript of a taped conversation between Barry Sullivan and R. J. Sells (in the author's files).
8 Alan Sullivan, letter to R. J. Sells, undated (in the author's files).

The Savage Club Sells refers to is the club to which Sullivan belonged, located on Carlton House Terrace in London—a typical London club, restricted to men only, the gathering place of writers, publishers, and the like. It was here that Alan rubbed shoulders with the well-known men of letters of the time and also here that he escaped from family life. Sullivan was a man of considerable wit, a brilliant conversationalist, and a gentleman—the necessary attributes of a good club member. All in all, Sullivan must have enjoyed these fourteen years of country life, generously sprinkled with trips to London and abroad. They were certainly productive years for his writing.

In 1926 four books were published. *Under Northern Lights*, a collection of eleven stories about the Canadian north, emphasized the grim atmosphere in which man "survives only by the stoutness of his heart and the strength of his body."[9] In these stories Sullivan advances two major ideas: first, that technological advance destroys the balance within nature; second, that Indians and Eskimos are not inferior to, but different from, other races. A constant theme in Sullivan's writing of Northern Canada, that of survival, is stressed repeatedly. European ignorance of the native way of life is ridiculed in "Trade" and "The Reward of Swasind." Most of the conflicts are resolved by physical battles, as in "The Circuit of the Wild Swans," where the leader battles another male for a female of the species.

Human Clay, published under the pseudonym Sinclair Murray and with B. V. Shann, his friend from the Savage Club, as co-author, was a first venture by Sullivan into science fiction. It received good reviews and sold well. *In The Beginning*, also science fiction, was published under Sullivan's own name. The plot revolves around John Caxton, an English scientist, whose only daughter Jean, cannot decide whether she loves Gregory Burden, a big game hunter, or Philip Sylvester, a student of flora and fauna. After explaining that she was "looking at two men who [had] never been tested"[10] and that "they generally test themselves,"[11] Caxton proposes that the three of them accompany him on a scientific expedition to Chile. He had received a letter from a fellow scientist

---

9   Alan Sullivan, *Under the Northern Lights* (London: J. M. Dent, 1926), p. 9.
10   Alan Sullivan, *In The Beginning* (London: Hurst and Blackett, 1926), p. 9.
11   Ibid., p. 10.

telling of seeing the body of what had been considered to be an extinct prehistoric monster, a giant ground sloth, the Megatherium. They discover a valley in Patagonia which, by a freak of natural climate, had survived in the primeval state, complete with prehistoric animals and men, which Caxton describes in terms of the Garden of Eden. Burden seems to be a throwback to the primeval men and becomes their leader after first agreeing to Caxton's plan to preserve the whole area as a museum for mankind. There is clever movement back and forth between civilized man and prehistoric man, in the mind of Burden, until, as a result of the introduction of the gift of fire to prehistoric man, the valley is destroyed. Underlying the story is the Sullivan theme of "the test," to isolate the essence of man. Sylvester passes the test and wins Jean.

The Days of Their Youth was dedicated to "the Two Kathleens," Sullivan's sister and his daughter. Set in Surrey and London in the early twenties, the story is about the Rennet family. John leaves Oxford to be an engineer, and Gertie has a career in real estate. The father, Paul Rennett, who has died before the action begins, remains as a disembodied spirit who watches over the others with unemotional objectivity. The only character who continues a relationship with the father after his death is his daughter Julia, a budding artist. John, after escaping from Oxford into engineering, makes another move toward independence from the past by emigrating to Canada. The movement in the story is of struggle to escape from the past toward a new life in the future; there is some "avant-garde" treatment of careers for women and, in the character of John, some of Sullivan's own spirit of independence. Most of the conflicts in the work are internal, as each character attempts to "find himself."

In 1927 four more books by Sullivan were published. One of these, *The Verdict of the Sea*, is a love story set in Wales. The other three have at least part of their settings in Canada and are related to Canadian life. *Brother Blackfoot* takes place in the Rocky Mountains when Indians were first being subjected to the white man's way of life. Sullivan writes of Natakina, Chief of the Blackfoot Tribe, of John Hartop, the American who wishes to be an engineer, and of Apau, who wishes to forsake the life-style of his forefathers to be a grocer. Sanders, a mining engineer, the man whom Hartop emulates, is probably Sullivan himself. The essential Sullivan tends to appear in two ways: in presenting an example of his ideal man and, through description of the natural surroundings, Sullivan's understanding and love of nature. The natural struggle is illustrated here in the fight to death between the lone grey wolf and the mountain lion.

The Splendid Silence begins with Duncan Seymour, the hero leaving Moat House in England to go to the rugged wilderness of British Columbia. Seymour's motive for leaving England is the questionable past of his young stepmother, Marian, and his father's mistaken idea that the son loves her. In British Columbia Seymour works in a lumber camp, part of the estate inherited by Miss Sydney Cartwright, which is beset with labour unrest caused by the Industrial Workers of the World, who attack and wound Seymour. Seymour and Sydney become engaged, and are welcomed back to Moat House after all misunderstandings are overcome. Duncan Seymour, however, loves the wilderness:

> . . . this cloistered wilderness became populated with wraiths of the lightfooted tribes who, now long vanished, once tenanted these deserted groves. . . . The picture seemed to catch his breath. It made him long to be immortal, to live, not for a few years of hunger and passion, but for ever and ever.[12]

Sydney and Duncan live half of each year in England and half in British Columbia. The title has a dual meaning, referring to the atmosphere of the wilderness and to Duncan's deliberate silence about Marian.

Whispering Lodge was described in *The Times* of London as "a pleasant and ingeniously spun yarn." The *Manchester Guardian* called it "an excellent tale, with an abundance of exciting incident." *The Aberdeen Press* referred to it as "a thriller that will take some beating . . . piquant situations, deftly portrayed." On the opening page of the novel a statement by Tonia Charters which refers to England could easily have been made by Sullivan: "it all looks predestined and so tidy. As if people had been staying for years putting the place in order."[13] Seen through the eyes of the major character, Tonia, the plot concerns her brother Julian and his friend Rodney, who leaves Oxford to continue his education in

---

12 Alan Sullivan, *The Splendid Silence* (New York: Dutton, 1927), p. 186.
13 Sinclair Murray (pseud.), *Whispering Lodge* (Toronto: Ryerson, 1927), p. 1.

Toronto where he falls in love with Tonia and with Canada. The Charters family do the reverse of what Rodney has done: they leave Canada for an inherited home in England. Mr. Charters is described as feeling "like an expatriate whose forebears had left England and crossed the sea a hundred years ago. He began to feel that in some other life some part of him had lived here."[14] The lodge to which they move in Kent and the life surrounding it is important, more for its reflection of Sullivan's understanding of the contrast between life in Canada and that in England, than for its contribution to the mysterious and romantic plot. The lodge is Sheerland House, which Sullivan had described as "Whispering Lodge" because of the mysterious sounds in its cavernous kitchens and basement storerooms.

Although this was the height of Sullivan's "English Period," three of the four books published in 1927 are closely related to Sullivan's experiences in Canada and reflect his desire to be back there. Although he officially lived outside Canada for twenty years, spiritually the exile was short-lived, as is evident when we note that Sullivan's major Canadian novels began to be published five years before his return to Canada in 1940. In addition, by 1935, although his home was Sheerland House, some months of each year were spent in Canada.

The years in England left Sullivan quite free to write and to travel. Kathleen was happily married and on her own; D'Arcy was in Zanzibar, Natalie was continuing her education and becoming involved in Conservative Party politics, Barry and Michael were at school and then at university. In 1928, for example, Sullivan was in Corsica where he took part in a boar hunt with the local men, and in October of the same year was in Canada to visit his mother and to stay at Government House in Ottawa. He did not return to Kent until Christmas Eve.

During this year only one book was published, *John Frensham K.C.,* written under the pseudonym Sinclair Murray, with B. V. Shann as joint author. The London *Daily Telegraph* described it as "a work of unusual power. The characters are excellently drawn, the dialogue well done." Until 1935 Sullivan's life appears to have followed much the same pattern; from January 1, 1929 until the end of 1934 he had seventeen books published,

---

14   Ibid., p. 3.

as well as short stories and articles, and he continued to travel, both in Europe and America.

Natalie, the second daughter of Alan and Bessie was an excellent scholar, educated in both England and France. She became fluent in French and was drawn toward political life. The announcement of her engagement to the Honourable Quinton Hogg, eldest son of the Right Honourable Viscount Hailsham, attracted considerable publicity, as did the marriage in 1932. Pictures of the couple at the time show her to be fashionably dressed and very beautiful. She worked actively in Hogg's political campaign of 1938, when he was first elected to the British House of Commons; she was very popular in his constituency and probably helped him considerably in his political career. The marriage ended in divorce in 1942, when Quinton Hogg was in the Middle East and after she met François Coulet, who had come to London with De Gaulle after the fall of France. Coulet was the chief of De Gaulle's cabinet in London and was one of the first government leaders to return to Normandy. After the war, Coulet served as French Ambassador to Finland, Syria, and Yugoslavia.

Bessie Sullivan enjoyed an active social life throughout these years, but it is the feeling of all four children that she probably would have been happiest had Sullivan been the type of author who was willing to be lionized by society; this would have enabled her to be the centre of a literary salon. He was not that type of man. Sullivan did, however, in his own way, mingle with other literary figures in England. It was either through the Pen Club or the Savage Club that he first met Basil Liddell Hart, the famous British Historian, military strategist, and expert on the life of T. E. Lawrence. For many years Sullivan carried on a correspondence with Liddell Hart, when they could not meet regularly to discuss Sullivan's writing. Alan respected Liddell Hart's point of view and sought his advice. (According to his children, he rarely sought their opinion of his writing; Bessie's criticism was largely disapproval of anything that she found to be "in bad taste.") It was through his friendship with Liddell Hart that his daughter Kathleen met her future second husband. When her first husband, Dr. Tim Nelson, was still alive she wrote to Liddell Hart inviting him to speak to a club at the hospital where her husband was a surgeon. The subject of his talk was to be T. E. Lawrence. In 1942 Kathleen married Liddell Hart, who was later knighted.

The seventeen books published by Sullivan in the six years between the end of 1928 and 1935 cannot all be treated in the same way. It would be unusual if they could; any author who publishes in quantity will have books which are best forgotten. What is important is that in his development he learns from his mistakes, and that later books improve in quality. It should also be remembered that some of Bessie Sullivan's fortune was lost in the 1929 stock market crash. As was the case with Sir Walter Scott, it became a financial necessity for Alan Sullivan to produce popular fiction to maintain the standard of living to which his family had become accustomed.

The term "popular fiction" raises a very difficult problem when assessing the work of a prolific writer and especially one belonging to a period of time now past; this difficulty has already been mentioned in the preface to this work. Part of the problem lies in the fact that popular fiction is not simply a literary phenomenon; popular fiction is only one facet of the popular culture which has evolved in Western civilization. The genesis and development of this culture is probably better explained in sociological and historical terms than in literary ones.

In a pamphlet *Notes on a Rationale for Popular Culture*, Russell B. Nye has briefly summarized the evolution of popular culture in our society. He begins with the idea that the arts that have the most validity for the greatest part of the population are not considered arts at all. Nye then proceeds to explain that popular culture began to appear in Western civilization in the late eighteenth century as one of the consequences of the industrial and democratic revolutions of that and later historical periods:

> It was one of a number of responses to the new kinds of social, political, and intellectual relationships that these revolutions involved.
>
> One of the conditions for the swift growth of popular culture in the later eighteenth century was a great explosion of population in Europe and the Americas, lasting well into the nineteenth, and its subsequent concentration into urban or semi-urban units which possessed unifying common social, economic, and cultural characteristics. As a result, there suddenly appeared a huge market with a tremendous desire for entertainment and the wealth to satisfy it. . . .
>
> Another factor in the rise of popular culture was the emergence, at about the same time, of a middle class, rapidly

democratizing society. As the upper classes gradually lost control of cultural standards, the spread of education and literacy through the great middle class created a new kind of audience, predicated on the median tastes of the population at large.... This mass society had leisure time, money, and cultural unity; it needed a new art—neither folk nor elite—to instruct and entertain it.

. . . .

The growth of this large popular audience ... provided an unparalleled opportunity for artists who were willing to and could satisfy its cultural needs.... The popular artist made his own tradition by calculating what the public wanted and evolving ways and means (some adapted from folk art) for giving it to them. In other words, the artist who wrote for this audience turned professional (as Daniel Defoe did), creating for profit the kind of art that the public was willing to buy.

. . . .

Popular art.... is a calculated attempt to meet the audience's expectations....

High or "elite" art, on the other hand, is produced by known artists within a consciously aesthetic context under the authority of an accepted set of rules; its success or failure is judged in relation to an established, normative tradition which both artist and audience know and respect.

. . . .

This does not mean that what the popular artist does is not worth doing, or personally unsatisfying, or aesthetically bad, or commercially cheap.... But it does mean that popular art, to be successful, has to be immediately popular; the mass public will not wait very long to be entertained, nor will it work hard at it.[15]

According to Nye's analysis of popular culture one could define popular fiction simply as that fiction which the public likes and is willing to pay for. I hasten to interject, however, as I have stated in the preface, that popular fiction and literary fiction are not necessarily mutually exclusive forms of writing. A popular novel may have considerable literary merit.

To a certain extent Sullivan could be described as being a schizophrenic writer; this is symbolized, perhaps, by his use of the pseudonym Sinclair Murray. Sullivan, at certain times in his career, wrote to appeal to popular taste; at other times he could

---

15   Russell B. Nye, *Notes on a Rationale for Popular Culture* (Bowling Green, Ohio: Popular Culture Association, 1970), pp. 1-10.

afford to strive for a higher standard of art. In this study, with few exceptions, I have emphasized those novels which I believe aspire to being "high art." Those that I merely mention in passing are probably those which Sullivan himself would have been the first person to identify as "pot-boilers." But I recognize that my opinion, and even Sullivan's opinion, of his fiction are subjective. The final judgement of a work of fiction, as of any work of art, may lie sometimes with the critics, sometimes with the readers, sometimes with time, or any combination of these. For example, *Judith* by Aritha van Herk, was recently named the first winner of a fifty-thousand dollar prize for a first novel by a Canadian writer. Yet one is inclined to agree with Douglas Hill's criticism of *Judith*:

> Judith is a competent work, frequently impressive in its descriptions of the exotic, but its core isn't hot. Too much of the passion and feeling and nuance van Herk seems to be reaching for remains abstraction, distanced by the very techniques and devices she has counted so heavily upon. Emotion has been turned into form, not liberated and given shape by form. Perhaps it's simply a matter of limited imagination or talent; fairer, I think, to consider that the problem lies with a type of novel—in a too familiar tradition—that now needs more than mere competence to catch fire.[16]

Perhaps, five (or fifty) years from now someone will ask, "Who decided to give an award to *Judith*?" And perhaps others will wonder why a popular work such as Segal's *Love Story* and its sequel were not recognized as works of art with a subtle classical pattern woven into the fabric of fiction.

When Sullivan wrote fiction to appeal to popular taste he produced works of historical romance, mystery, melodrama, adventure, and love. Ironically, perhaps, at the time when Sullivan was doing his writing there had been for some time a popular interest in stories of the Canadian west and north. Gilbert Parker, for example, although he had no real experience of either area, produced, with regularity, novels about these areas. Sullivan, in writing of the Canadian west and north, was not simply appealing to the public's appetite, but was "bodying forth in works of art his response to those primeval environments" (to paraphrase a statement by Frederick Philip Grove). Two of the books published by

---

16 Douglas Hill, "Gritted Teeth on The Pig Farm," a review of Aritha van Herk, *Judith*, in *Saturday Night* 93 (November, 1978), pp. 67-68.

Sullivan in 1929 have settings in these areas of Canada. *The Story of One-Ear* and *The Training of Chiliqui* are parts of a series of readers for schools. The first is about an Eskimo dog and the second about an Indian boy.

The Story of One-Ear is an imaginative piece of writing for young people, giving a clear picture of life in the Arctic through the eyes of a Husky, who received his name from having had one ear bitten off early in his life. The life of the dog and that of a young Eskimo boy, Cunayou, are woven together in this tale which realistically dramatizes Eskimo life. The opening pages briefly create an impression of the setting:

> If you will look at a map of the Arctic, you will see a big stretch of water, shaped something like a banana, lying to the north of Hudson's Bay. On the west side of this is a large bit of land, shaped rather like a pear after the flies have got at it. This is Boothia Peninsula. And Aivick, the hunter, lived just where the stalk of the pear would come if it had one.
>
> We would call it a lonely place, but Aivick did not think so. Not a tree anywhere—therefore no firewood unless a bit of some wrecked ship were washed ashore. No grass, because the country was solid rock. A good deal of moss that the caribou ate with relish. In summer time—and Aivick did not like the summer because it made him perspire so much—the sun was very hot. The family was composed of Cunayou, an only son. Cunayou means "the Sculpin." If you have ever seen a sculpin, which is a fish with a mouth like a hole in a wall, you will understand how he got this name. His mother was called Allegoo, the Drinking Cup.[17]

Later we are given some understanding of the unique relationship between man and dog in the Arctic:

> Perhaps it would be well at this point to say that in the Arctic one cannot find a hunter without dogs—that the dogs are just as important as spear or fishing-line or gun—and there exists between dogs and man something rather different from that which one finds in other parts of the world. If the dogs are hungry it means that the hunter is also short of food. If the dogs are happy the master is the same.[18]

Much of the success of the story results from the clever development of the relationship of One-Ear and Cunayou as they face

different experiences together, the last of which involves the boy
and the dog succeeding in bringing help for the boy's father,
Aivick. Throughout the narrative Sullivan reveals his precise
knowledge of the Eskimo life-style and philosophy; this is clearly
illustrated in his references to the sharing of food:

> It is one of the laws of the north that when there is meat in camp it
> is shared equally by all. Thus there can be no such thing as full
> stomachs in one igloo, and empty ones in another close by. The law
> applies to relations, friends and strangers, and it has happened
> before this that when an enemy asked for food it was given without
> hesitation.[19]

The Training of Chiliqui is the story of an Indian boy from age
one until he is a youth. At the end of the story Chiliqui saves the
life of a young engineer who is obviously Sullivan himself. The
story begins near Lake Nipigon, north of Lake Superior, one of the
first areas visited by Alan Sullivan with his father after they moved
to Sault Ste. Marie and the area to which Sullivan returned when he
had to leave the University of Toronto. His knowledge of Indian
life emerges clearly in this well-developed narrative. Sullivan
writes of Chiliqui at age eleven:

> There were certain things that the boy had been taught, and
> perhaps the most important was to remember what he saw. For an
> Indian this means everything, because the only maps these brown-
> skinned people have are the ones they carry in their own heads. So
> at once Chiliqui began to take notes without pencil or paper,
> chewing at the fish, which was not very well cooked, spitting out
> bones, counting the islands in sight, photographing in the back of
> his head the shape and height of the hills, the colour and size of the
> rocks, the tracks of animals in the sand, the direction of the clouds
> and wind—which is not always the same—and, altogether, ob-
> serving a large number of things that would have entirely escaped
> you and me. When he had digested this, as well as all of the fish
> except head and tail, he heard the squeal of a rabbit in the snare,
> took it out, loaded up, and paddled on as lightly as a feather drifts
> across a pool. Can you see him—this eleven-year-old Ojibway boy,
> with his bright, observant eyes, his copper-coloured skin, his slim,
> active body, his long rather thin hands, his very white teeth, alone
> on the first solitary journey of life?[20]

---

19 Ibid., p. 40.
20 Alan Sullivan, *The Training of Chiliqui* (London: George Philip and Son,
    1929), pp. 14-15.

The other two books by Sullivan published in 1929, *The Broken Marriage* and *Double Lives*, written under his pseudonym Sinclair Murray, are simple love stories. *Queer Partners*, also by Sinclair Murray and published in 1930, uses images related to gambling to symbolize life as a game of chance. When a man named Tarrant is believed to have drowned, his partner, Jackson, persuades the widowed Mrs. Tarrant to take her yacht, *Cygnet*, to South Africa to retrieve some diamonds. Throughout the book the references to gambling and to the analogy of life as a gamble include frequent use of the term "bluffing." A major example of bluffing is the faked drowning of Tarrant. The title refers to a series of queer partnerships which form and then break up; despite the temporary relationships the characters remain isolated. The yacht itself is isolated, except for its link by radio with the outside world. Even this link is gone when Jackson throws it overboard. Aside from the setting on the yacht, the background is England.

In 1930 Sullivan published, under his own name *A Little Way Ahead*. In this novel the hero, Felix Marbury, wishes to escape from his job behind a desk in a London brokerage firm to seek wealth and power. He discovers that he is able to experience visions which tell what will happen on the stock market; as a result he acquires the reputation of a great speculator. As his wealth increases he tries to satisfy his wife with diamonds, and spends less and less time with her. After he fails financially, he thinks about what has happened: "Power came his way and he used it not for anyone's good but his own whims and aggrandisement. He might have done much, done anything; but in actuality, he only piled up power on power, till the pyramid got top-heavy, fell over, and crushed him."[21] The fall of Felix illustrates a major didactic theme in Sullivan. In his search for the ideal man, Sullivan sometimes points out the negative aspects rather than the positive. Felix is surrounded by people who wear masks to deceive him; they make use of his money and power in their own quest for the same ends. The contrasting characters are Felix's wife and Bruce McLeod, who has a dream for which he is willing to work in Honduras in the mines to achieve happiness.

Mr. Absalom, also published in 1930, is a well-written thriller, one of those books Sullivan was able to turn out to produce income to support his family. By far the best novel of the eight

---

21   Alan Sullivan, *A Little Way Ahead* (Toronto: Macmillan, 1930), p. 310.

published in 1929 and 1930, and perhaps the only one of genuine merit from those years, is *The Magic Makers*. Sergeant Jock Mactier, a retired member of the R.C.M.P. who has served for years in the Canadian Arctic, sees an advertisement in an Edinburgh paper requiring a person with his experience. He accepts the challenge offered: to find Henry Rintoul, who has left for Canada after being cut out of his father's will for wishing to marry a girl of whom the father does not approve. The father dies before changing his will and before learning that the fiancee was a woman of considerable integrity. Henry passes through Montreal, Cobalt, and on to the Arctic. The clue to his whereabouts is a message received on a piece of soft, tanned hide. Jock attempts to follow the map on the hide, with the help of Nanook, an Eskimo. The title refers to the fact that because first Henry, and then Jock, can create shocks with electric batteries the Eskimo people think that they "make magic." We learn that when Henry's batteries had gone dead, he was cast out, and he became the leader of a wolf pack. This, of course, is a bizarre element in the story, but the realistic atmosphere of the Arctic is accurately created, and the story is so well-written that one submits to a "willing suspension of disbelief." Henry and Jock both escape after using dynamite to create impressive magic. The novel proves that when Sullivan writes of the areas he knows and loves, he succeeds in writing a good story. Sullivan's own feelings emerge strongly when he writes of Jock's being "lifted [inspired], and then flooded back on him all the mystery and appeal, all the voiceless fascination, all the vast invitation of the North."[22]

In 1931, three novels by Sullivan were published: *Golden Foundling*, *The Ironmaster*, and *No Secrets Island*. All three can be described as entertaining and, at times, exciting stories, but *The Ironmaster* has added interest. The book is an excellent example of Sullivan's ability to integrate interesting autobiographical material with purely imaginative fiction. It also illustrates Sullivan's skill in presenting a theme without explicitly defining it; here the theme usually emerges naturally from the dialogue and actions of the characters. Finally, the novel, with its setting completely in England, is a sample of the good writing done by Sullivan in his "English period."

---

22 Alan Sullivan, *The Magic Makers* (London: J. Murray, 1930), p. 11.

In the first paragraph of the book, young John Driver is introduced with information about his having attended a school in Scotland, the details of which parallel exactly Sullivan's own school, Loretto.

It was a famous school, and with those who knew no better it had the reputation of being a hard one. The buildings, low and grey, were a few hundred yards from an arm of the North Sea, and the Pentland Hills lifted not far to the south-east. Young John Driver was sent there at the age of thirteen, took to the life like a seal to salt water, and finished at eighteen as head of the school and Captain of the Fifteen. Cricket he considered rather futile, and never took to it seriously.[23]

Before leaving school young Driver meets with the Headmaster who obviously understands the boy's character:

"You're a Spartan, but the Spartans overdid things occasionally, and I'm inclined to think that later on you're going to be overhard on yourself."

"Myself!" blurted John.

"It's quite possible. There's such a thing as being contented without enjoying oneself, and one can realize one's ambition without attaining any great happiness. I don't know as much about steel as your grandfather does—or possibly you do yourself—but, offhand, I'd say you were tempered a bit too hard for general purposes." He smiled again. "There's such a thing as mild steel, isn't there?"[24]

The reference to the grandfather is to James Driver, who owns a large steel works. James has planned that John will marry Meg Burstall, whose family owns the coal mines which supply the fuel for his steel works. It is obvious that Sullivan's experience in the steel works at Sault Ste. Marie had a direct influence on much of the content of this novel. This becomes clear as John's character and life-style are presented. There are frequent examples of parallels with the character of Francis Clergue.

Meg has loved John since she was a little girl, but he remains completely oblivious of this fact. He thinks only of steel:

"Have you never thought what you'll do with your life?" Her lips trembled a little.

23 Alan Sullivan, *The Ironmaster* (London: J. Murray, 1931), p. 1.
24 Ibid., p. 9.

"I'm thinking of it all the time. There are the works—they'll keep me busy. Grandfather says I've got to master them before I own them. That will take years and years. It'll be a bit of a job, but I'm ready for it. And of course I won't marry for ever so long. Awful mistake for a chap to marry too young when he has a heap of other things to think about. Don't you agree?"

"It depends so much on—on the chap, doesn't it?"

John thought there might be something in this in the case of a chap who needed stiffening up, the sort of stiffening one could get by being responsible for someone else, and knowing that if one didn't succeed they would both be down and out. Personally, he didn't feel that way, and wanted to be free to devote himself entirely to his job till he had the job running like clockwork. And he was lucky in that the money side of it was all right, anyway.[25]

There is one obvious intrusion by the author, relating to Sullivan's theme of "the test" in connection with the quest for the essential qualities of man:

> Some natures are so constituted that difficulties do but inspire them, and each successive test breeds in some mysterious fashion the courage and spirit with which to face it. Thus it was with young John Driver. A month passed—then a year—then more years. He grew bigger, stronger, harder. He lived for the works. Everything in him responded to their gigantic mechanical creations. In their naked massiveness he found beauty, and inspiration in their titanic power. His chin became a bit more dominant, his lips more firmly set.[26]

John Driver continues in this pattern until he meets a friend of Meg's, Auriol Burt, a pretty and vivacious young socialite; he is immediately infatuated with her, and decides that she will be his wife. As John starts to tell his grandfather of his plans, the old man assumes that it is Meg he is speaking of, and blurts out his dream—his vision—of the merger of the steel and coal works by the marriage of the two young people:

> John's brain had begun to swim. He blinked. Old James had straightened his shoulders, and was standing, eyes half shut, as though peering at something. He seemed to be having a vision. Then he looked at John, who might have been, so far as the look went, new and strange and oddly significant.

---

25 Ibid., p. 25.
26 Ibid., p. 31.

"Driver iron from Burstall coal! Lad, lad, you've turned the trick at last! Now 'twill be Driver iron and Driver coal!"[27]

In reaction against the dream of his grandfather, John persuades Auriol to go with him to London where they marry. After a honeymoon, he leaves her behind, while he goes home to tell old James, who is eighty-two years of age. On hearing the news, James has a stroke and dies.

The marriage is doomed from the beginning. John, a multimillionaire, becomes the Ironmaster, and places his wife second to the steel works. She goes to London, where she renews her friendship with Tony Tennant, who had always loved her. John finds them together and asks for a legal separation. At the beginning of the World War I, Tennant enlists and goes to France; Meg becomes a nurse; Auriol works as a volunteer in a canteen; and John remains wedded to the works. Only after Meg has overcome her love for Driver and married Tennant, and after Auriol has been badly disfigured by a bomb in London, does John become a man and not just the Ironmaster:

> In that moment the Ironmaster became fused. He melted. He grew ductile. The hard, stubborn nature yielded, and the warmth of what lay against his cheek reaching his heart, charged it with an infinite pity and tenderness.[28]

In the epilogue of the novel, Sir John Driver is seen at the Fathers' and Sons' Cricket Match at Fonthorn school; with the change of three letters Fonthorn becomes Fonthill, and Driver becomes Sullivan playing cricket with his sons Barry and Michael. In this book about the Ironmaster, Sullivan has clearly demonstrated his belief that it is essential for men like Driver and Clergue, the industrialists, to keep their human side alive and separate from their ambition and drive.

Sullivan's publishing career continued unabated in the early part of the 1930s. In 1932 three more novels appeared. The first, *Antidote*, written under the Murray pseudonym, is the story of Thalia, an amoral, seductive woman who succeeds in hurting many others without being hurt herself. *Colonel Pluckett*, published under Sullivan's own name, is another of those love stories

---

27   Ibid., p. 83.
28   Ibid., p. 336.

Sullivan turned out to produce income to support the family; its setting is the Riviera. The most substantial of the three, *Cornish Interlude*, by Murray, is an interesting, well-written novel set in Cornwall. As David Jones, whose father has been lost at sea, is about to leave his mother to go to sea himself, he rescues a drowning woman from a ship-wrecked yacht. The woman asks that her presence in the village be kept a secret. There she meets Black Paul, who is competing with David for Lillian Treganna. The woman rescued by David—and the heroine of the story— turns out to be an opera singer, Josephine Bradley, who had decided on the spur of the moment to jilt Sir John Charwell, a lawyer, to run off with the owner of the yacht. When she learns that Paul is wanted for a murder he did not commit, she goes to Sir John and promises to marry him if he will defend Paul. He proves that Paul is innocent, and frees Josephine from her promise.

Of the two books published in 1933, *What Fools Men Are* and *Man at Lone Tree*, the first is by far the more interesting. It foreshadows the clouds of war which, within a few years, began to descend on Europe. It is about two miniature countries, Aricia and Sardosa, and the war which almost breaks out between them because the citizens of Aricia are accused of defacing the ugly statue of the founder of Sardosa given by its citizens to the other country as a token of friendship. This is one of the books about which Sullivan asked Liddell Hart's advice. He had "Sinclair Murray" change it into a script for a film in 1935. The prefatory note to that script stated that "the theme of this story might well apply to the international situation of today—to show the action of mass psychology—to show how humanity is swayed by unreasoning reactions to hopes, fears and rumour—to show how little men have learned from the past."[29] A touch of Sullivan in the story is the new type of airplane developed by the Aricians.

The most devastating word applied to some of Sullivan's fiction is "ephemeral." It accurately describes *The Obstinate Virgin*, the only novel published by Sullivan in 1934.

4

In 1935 Alan Sullivan entered a new phase in his publishing career. Although he continued to live at Sheerland House in Kent

---

29 Prefatory note to film script of *What Fools Men Are*.

until 1940, he spent more and more of his time in Canada, and almost all of his writing was about Canada. In addition, the major events in his private life were connected with his Canadian writing. He seems to have suddenly broken free from England and to have remained free of it until his death. As he had become increasingly involved in writing for the contemporary British reading public, he had drifted further and further away from the excellence of *The Passing of Oul-I-But and Other Tales*, *Under Northern Lights*, and *The Rapids*. Fortunately, he returned to Canadian settings and content and earned a reputation as an excellent writer on both sides of the Atlantic. The final evaluation of his literary talent will be greatly influenced by the significant novels published after he was sixty-five years of age. It is to be hoped that his eight or ten excellent volumes of fiction will be used, not his eight or ten literary failures, when he is compared with Hugh MacLennan, or Gabrielle Roy, both of whom have published only seven novels. Like Wordsworth and many another literary figure before him, Sullivan made the mistake of publishing too much. Faced with financial necessity, however, it must have been difficult to make decisions based strictly on literary quality.

V

The Return to Canada

1

Although Alan Sullivan's official home continued to be Sheerland House, Kent, until 1940, he had, at least in his own mind, returned to Canada from the time he began to write *The Great Divide: A Romance of the Canadian Pacific Railway*. In 1936 *The Money Spinners* appeared under the name of Sinclair Murray; it was the last of his non-Canadian novels. *The Great Divide*, published in 1935, was the turning point in his career; it was the first of several books that clearly gave him a permanent place in the history of Canadian literature. John Stevenson has written that "it was a valuable service to Canada to embalm, as he did, in literary form so many great events in the history of the west, like the building of the C.P.R. through the Rockies, . . . Indian tales and famous characters among the pioneers along with notable episodes in their careers."[1]

When *The Great Divide* was published, it received excellent critical response. Janet Munro, for example, wrote a lengthy review in *Saturday Night*, which concludes by stating that "magnificent descriptions of men and scenery vivify the episodes in the book."[2] The work—as novel and as film—went under various

---

1   John A. Stevenson, "Alan Sullivan, Poet, Engineer," *Saturday Night* 62 (August 23, 1947), 25.

2   Janet Munro, "Building the C.P.R.," review of *The Great Divide* in *Saturday Night* 50 (October 19, 1935), 10.

titles. Sullivan first called it *Track of Destiny*; he then changed the title to *The Great Divide*. Later it was filmed as *The Great Barrier*, in England, and in Canada the film was called *Silent Barriers*.

The first chapter of the book is brilliant writing. Beginning with a detailed description of the Roger's Pass in summer, and then a parallel description in winter, Sullivan gradually introduces Apau ("the weasel") and his wife, She of the Pretty Head, and their child, Light in the Morning. It is beautifully designed symbolism; Apau hunts for food to sustain his wife and child, and succeeds in tracking and killing a moose; Apau, in turn, is killed by a grizzly bear, who then carries off the moose. The combination of the description of the primeval setting and the tone of the narrative, conveying an absolute acceptance of the harshness of the natural cycle, sets the stage for the major narrative of the book—the building of the railroad—which, symbolic of man's progress, destroys the balance of nature for people like Apau and many others. Like Ethel Wilson's use of the battle between the eagle and the osprey in a much later book, *Swamp Angel*, also set in British Columbia, the opening chapter of *The Great Divide* presents the unchangeable pattern of life as established by nature. The narrative of the building of the railroad is enhanced when read in light of this symbolic pattern; it achieves incandescence, to use Ethel Wilson's terminology.

The political and financial facts of the building of the C.P.R., which are now common knowledge to us, were very accurately presented by Sullivan in 1935. He had undertaken considerable research before writing the book; in addition he was able to add a dimension that is lacking in later books about the same episode in our history. Sullivan's personal experience with the C.P.R., although at a later date than the building of the railway through the Rockies, gave him the capacity to capture the atmosphere of the camps and the character of the men who worked on the railway itself. Although the love story between Big John Hickey and Mary Moody is, as Janet Munro has said, "more or less thrown in,"[3] it does help Sullivan to integrate imaginary characters realistically in order to fill out the drama of the building of the railroad. John is also intended by Sullivan to present in microcosm the spirit of the Canadian nation in this great undertaking. That interpretation illuminates the following passage:

3 Ibid.

The truth was, though he could not apprehend it, he had journeyed out of his old useless rut into a new sphere of influence. Divorced from all he had hitherto known and seen, he now yielded insensibly to that primitive pressure of the wilderness which turns the mind of man in upon itself in search of something suspected to be there but not yet disclosed, and he was about to evidence the fact that while man makes things it is equally certain that things may make men. Not yet was he made: there remained still too much of the old casual self for that, but he had a sense of release, an instinct not before uncovered, and the stirrings of that self-awareness which is the precursor of action. Big John was of the raw material from which the all-red line was destined to fashion many into complete manhood: no small affair of trade and profit could do this, for it took nothing less than the stand-up battle between humanity and the untamed forces of nature.

So what with this, and the curious effect of following the snake that could not die, and encountering so many who knew and had seen so much more than himself, he acquired a sort of humility, out of which grew the desire to have something to do with what must be certainly the biggest thing in the world. People on the coast had been dubious and satirical as to the line ever being finished. One knew better now.[4]

The historical setting of the novel is Sir John A. MacDonald's return to power, when two thousand miles of the railway still remained to be built. Sullivan believed that if it had not been for the promise given by MacDonald to British Columbia, the Rockies would have been Canada's western boundary and the United States would own the whole western coast of North America. As soon as MacDonald was back in power he had made it financially possible for the railway construction to be carried on. The characters of MacDonald, Tupper, and the other political figures are presented with historical accuracy, but what is equally important to the success of the novel is that the reader is introduced to those individuals who survey the route, clear the land, lay the track, and provide necessities for the workers. Among these is a gambler, Kelly, The Rake, residing in Yale. Then, Big Mouth Kelly, the undertaker, is presented, as well as Graveyard. These three, along with Bulldog Kelly, Silent Kelly, Molly Kelly, and Long Kelly had gathered in Yale, on the banks of the Fraser, in order to benefit

---

4   Alan Sullivan, *The Great Divide* (London: Lovat Dickson and Thompson, 1935), p. 193.

from the half-million dollars Onderdonk had received from the government to blast his way up the Fraser in search of a supply route for the railroad.

Sullivan describes the inhabitants of Yale very thoroughly, from the three grades of prostitutes available to the workers, to the Oriental merchants and Jewish peddlers, and, of course, Jack Kirkup, "the single arm of the law, in helmet, brass buttons, tight-cut breeches, blue tunic, and truncheon. Jack carried no gun and occupied most of his time in depositing unconscious men behind woodpiles, or the favoured ones on heaps of empty gunny sacks."[5]

Sullivan successfully blends historical accuracy with his own imaginative fiction. This is true of his introduction into the story of James J. Hill, "the master railway builder of the continent,"[6] Van Horne, laying track across the prairies, "Hell's Bells" Major Rogers, who started at Kamloops and looked for a short cut through the Selkirks, and Donald Smith, the financier. The completion of the building of the line with the driving of the last spike is described near the end of the novel in a letter from John Hickey to Mary. This low-key approach to a moment of history is in keeping with Sullivan's treatment of the whole story; he did not write *The Great Divide* as a potential television spectacular or as a historical document.

Sullivan's *The Great Divide*, published in 1935, cannot be compared with the two massive volumes, *The National Dream* and *The Last Spike*, assembled by Pierre Berton and assorted research assistants, with the co-operation of government agencies, libraries, archives, newspapers, and many other sources. These books published in 1970 and 1971, with the copyright held by Pierre Berton Enterprises Ltd., are to Sullivan's novel what satellite television coverage now is to shortwave radio of 1935. On the other hand, one can draw a comparison between Sullivan's novel and E. J. Pratt's narrative poem, "Towards the Last Spike." In his brilliant poem, Pratt, like Sullivan, takes an understated approach to the driving of the last spike. Sullivan's description of the event follows:

Well, miss, yesterday I saw the last spike driven and it wasn't as exciting as you'd think being just a standard iron spike out of the

5   Ibid., p. 44.
6   Ibid., p. 60.

keg. It was like this, Van Horne had come up with a carfull of big bugs from the east and I saw them all a lot of them had beaver hats but not Van Horne or Ross or Dan Mann. Dan hadn't any hat. There was a tall man with a long square beard that was Fleming and Tom Wilson had told me about him the evening before we hit the Lake of Little Fishes, and your friend Mr. Smith who put up the million, his beard was white, and Hell's Bells and a lot of track-layers and my gang and a water boy.

The grade was all ready and we could see Onderdonk's men working up the pass slamming down rails as fast as they could and spiking while we were doing the same till there was just twenty feet left open. Everyone was kind of quiet and quit talking so you could hear nothing but those last two rails getting sawed to length, and someone told me that Onderdonk's rails had come right round south America to the Fraser to get there to Eagle Pass in the Gold Range. It seemed a long way to come.

Well miss, when the rails were sawed off Onderdonk's gang took one end and mine the other and laid them in place then someone hands Mr. Smith a hammer and old Hell's Bells takes a spike and holds it right where it ought to go and looks up at Mr. Smith like as he was scared for his nuckels. I guess Mr. Smith is 70 years old and then some but he gives Van Horne a sort of frosty little smile takes a kind of half swing and darned if he didn't come down fair and square as if he'd done it all his life while Hell's Bells sat right there and laughs. I was kind of surprised but he drove her home good and tight into a spruce tie with an eight inch face which is standard. No one said a word while he was swinging and Hell's Bells was certainly relieved over his nuckels. The weather was dull and rainy but I guess it's going to turn colder.

Then someone started cheering but Mr. Smith didn't turn a hair, he keeps just as quiet as a January muskeg and says he thinks the whole job is very well done, and Van Horne allows that anyone who travels over that road will pay full fare, and right there they called the place some Scotch name that I can't spell but it's chalked on a board so I'll copy it out. Then the crowd from the east got aboard the private car with Onderdonk's gang of friends and started for the west with a lot on the back platform and us fellows waving our hats and it started to rain. I ain't quite used to the steel being down but I guess that'll come. Some fellows say right now that Onderdonk's road isn't up to our standard.[7]

---

7   Ibid., pp. 382-83.

2

In the summer of 1935 Sullivan travelled through British Columbia and the Canadian Arctic by air, land, and water. He returned to
Sheerland House in December. Five days after returning to England, Sullivan left again for Canada to select locations for the
filming of *The Great Barrier* by the Gaumont-British Picture
Corporation. By January 20 he was writing to Bessie about choos-
ing suitable sites in Revelstoke for the film. This must have been
an exciting time for Sullivan—at the age of sixty-seven to be back
in his beloved Canada, planning for the movie version of his novel
which had not yet been in print a year. In the summer of 1936 the
production crew arrived in Revelstoke to make the film—it was,
up to that date, the largest film production unit ever assembled in
Canada.

While the film was being made in Revelstoke, Sullivan again
travelled to the Arctic, this time right up to the Arctic Circle. He
had snapshots taken at Coronation Gulf in July, 1936 with Wiley
Post and Will Rogers; he was one of the last persons to see them
alive before their fatal plane crash in Point Barrow. While engaged
in these extensive travels he was, nonetheless, busy writing what
was to be some of his best fiction.

On February 4, 1937 the film *The Great Barrier* had its world
premiere at the Gaumont Theatre, London, in the presence of
Queen Mary. Also in the audience were Lord and Lady Strathcona.
Lady Strathcona wore a family heirloom, a diamond-set section of
the last spike which had been driven by Donald Smith, the first
Lord Strathcona. The following account of the event appeared in
the magazine, *Canada's Weekly*, on February 12, 1937:

> Her Majesty Queen Mary attended on February 4, in the new
> Gaumont Theatre, Haymarket, the world premiere of the new
> Gaumont-British film "The Great Barrier," which re-creates in
> sound-movie form the thrilling story of the building of the Cana-
> dian Pacific Railway. The premiere was held in aid of Mrs. Stanley
> Baldwin's "Safer Motherhood" appeal—the National Birthday
> Trust Fund for Extension of Maternity Services—and the financial
> result for the Fund was announced from the screen as 3,000
> pounds.
>
> Lord Strathcona is one of the Vice-Chairmen of the Fund, and
> he, the Hon. Vincent and Mrs. Massey, and Mr. Alan Sullivan
> (author of the story on which "The Great Barrier" is based), and

Mrs. Sullivan, were present as guests of Mr. J. C. Patteson (European manager, Canadian Pacific) and Mrs. Patteson. Among other distinguished members of the audience were: The Duchess of Buccleuch, the Marchioness of Anglesey, Sir Julien Cahn, Bt. Lady George Cholmondeley, Lady Violet Astor, the Countess of Bessborough, Lady Bird, Lady Margaret Boscawen, Viscountess Buckmaster, Viscountess Castlereagh, the Marchioness of Crewe, the Countess of Cromer, Mrs. Anthony de Rothschild, Mrs. Lionel de Rothschild, the Marchioness of Dufferin and Ava, the Countess of Ellesmere, Viscountess Fitzalan of Derwent, Lady Forres, Viscountess Greenwood, Viscountess Hailsham, Viscountess Hambleden, Lady Howard de Walden, the Countess of Iddesleight, the Marchioness of Londonderry, the Countess of Malmesbury, the Countess of Plymouth, the Marchioness of Salisbury, Mrs. Arthur Sassoon, Mrs. Mayer Sassoon, Lady Simon, Viscountess Wakefield, the Duchess of Westminster, and Gertrude, Lady Worthington-Evans.

The film has received enthusiastic praise from the critics, the Empire theme and the dramatic part played in it by the builders of the Canadian Pacific being especially recognised.[8]

In addition to the social success of the premiere, the movie itself received enthusiastic praise from the press. It was a great moment for Alan Sullivan, and perhaps an even greater one for his wife; it was the type of evening which she must have lived for.

The film, with the title changed to *Silent Barriers*, scored a triumph in Canada. According to a report in *The Edmonton Journal*, it broke all records for attendance at the Rialto Theatre in that City. Between noon of the Friday on which it opened and midnight of the same day, 5,762 persons saw it. *The Edmonton Journal* report was typical of other Canadian reviews of the film.

> Pictorially, it was breathtakingly magnificent . . . . Historically it brought to life on the screen an enduring and faithful record of the heroic achievement . . . . Dramatically the film stood solidly on its own merits as a powerful, simply-told story replete with all the elements of romance, comedy and gripping suspense.[9]

This recognition by Canadians gave Alan Sullivan inspiration to continue writing for the remaining ten years of his life.

---

8 Anon., "The Great Barrier," a review of the film in *Canada's Weekly*, London England, February 12, 1937.
9 C.W.G., "Rialto Feature Canadian Epic," *The Edmonton Journal*, April 4, 1937.

3

In 1938, the year in which Sullivan celebrated his seventieth birthday, he had three books published. *The Cycle of the North* is largely a selection of sketches published earlier in *Oul-I-But and Other Tales*; his trips to the Arctic in 1935 and 1936 obviously renewed his interest in this earlier writing. The title refers to the first sketch, which follows the seasons along the shores of Hudson Bay. The later sketches have men set against these stern surroundings. Although much of his intervening publishing had drifted far from this sort of writing, in speeches and articles he had expressed concern about the treatment of Canada's native people. For example, in June, 1937, he wrote a letter to *The Times* of London in reply to an article which had been critical of the treatment of Indian people by Canadian authorities. His letter, which would not be popular today, expressed with some candour the difficulties which faced those who were attempting to help the Indian people. Sullivan was aware, as perhaps few Canadians were at that time, of what the white man's civilization was doing to the native people. This is brought out very clearly in an address he delivered at a meeting in England:

> ... At this point it is necessary to make a clear distinction between the native tribes of the north as they were a few years ago, and as they are now. The complexion of their mentality has changed, and their primitive conceptions, if not altogether lost, are confused under the onrush of modernity. They have no words in which to describe things common to their new life. The Indian who reads the weather forecast, no longer believes in his father's gods of wind and rain.
>
> He does not understand—and what man of us does—the conflict of our creeds. He is apt to acquire our vices without our virtues, our diseases without our powers of resistance. The old gods have lost their dominion, and his mind bends under the display of new forces, administered by man, and which he will never understand. Thus if you ask me what the average primitive in North America believes today, I cannot tell you. Nor, I think, would anyone. But what he was is another story, and I can, perhaps, give you something of his mentality in those still recent years when a deity spoke to him through Baim-wa-wa, the Thunder, and Ani-mee-kee, the Lightning, was a gesture of anger from on high.
>
> The native tribes of Canada consist of Indians and Eskimo. These are the first families, and the dividing Line between them is

climatic rather than geographical, because the Indian dislikes cold, and the Eskimo heat. They do not fancy each other. The Indian, speaking broadly, is subjective, the Eskimo objective.

These races, before their discovery and spoliation by ourselves, shared most of the primitive virtues. They were brave, uncomplaining, generous. They were, and still are, devoted to their kindred. They had a shining honesty. Their word was their bond. Living, as most of them did, on the ragged edge of death, deceit or evasion was foreign from their thoughts. A man's hold on life, and the safety of his family, lay in the strength of his arm, the quickness of his eye. What he killed was not for his eating alone, it being the unwritten law that no stranger should go unsheltered or unfed.

Their wisdom was that of wind and water. They had microscopic powers of observation, developed to an extraordinary degree through how many ages, and felt by instinct a thousand emanations of nature. Wild life, furred and feathered, had no secrets from them, for on their understanding of this hung their very existence.

These qualities, and many more than it is now possible to describe, were shared alike by Indian and Eskimo. With them, something else. The unshakeable belief in a conscious and active existence after death.

One can only hazard the reason for such a belief. They do not give reasons. If one attempted to probe the subject, they would feel at a disadvantage, and answer with a look. Their father's father believed it—which is enough for them.

But apart from that it has always seemed to me that such a creed is the inevitable concomitant of a life of effort and uncertainty. These tribes dealt with realities from which there was no escape. By first principle, and the austere functioning of natural laws, they lived and died. The second principle assured them of something better, less tricky, less menacing. This was their second life. Thus from the rocky shores of Labrador to the cathedral forests of the Pacific slopes, from the Arctic to the Great Lakes, the creed was the same. Survival.

Might one suggest that a phase of this argument is applicable to ourselves, and reason that the man who on this earth is lethargic, casual, unanchored and undirected can have slight reason for anticipating another existence with any real interest? Why should he?[10]

---

10   Alan Sullivan, typescript of an address delivered (ca. 1935) to a women's organization in England which he referred to as "The League" and which was presided over by Mrs. Dawson Scott (in the author's files).

The second book published in 1938 was *With Love From Rachel*, by "Sinclair Murray"; in Canada it was published under the author's own name rather than the pseudonym. The story, which takes place in the Canadian Arctic, concerns Rachel Bedell, a quarter-breed, who has fallen in love with an Arctic pilot, Jack Wilding. Rachel's home, when she is not out on the trap line, is in Aklavik. Although Sullivan's female characters are not always successful, Rachel is an extremely well-drawn character. Early in the book she is introduced:

> She was a strange girl, a sort of composite creature, as much at home in a city as in the Arctic. To the city, where she dressed as did other women, she brought a sharp, wild tang of wilderness: men and women alike noted the erect body, the free lift of head, her poise and complete unconscious calm. She had excellent taste in clothes, accepted no advances, sold her fur in the best market, enjoyed herself in her own independent fashion, ignoring the interest she roused, then, having enough city, would return to Aklavik, on the delta of the Mackenzie, where she moved an equal amongst men, lay her winter trap lines, and catch fur with the best of them. She seemed happy. She confided in none except Wilding, and in the secret heart of her she loved him.[11]

The arrival in Aklavik of Paula Deming creates the eternal triangle. After much mystery and adventure, Rachel, as the result of a prophetic dream, saves the life of Jack, but she dies as a result of a bullet wound because she has concealed her wound until she has made certain that Jack is looked after at the outpost hospital. It is then too late to do anything for her.

The final book published by Sullivan in 1938 was *The Fur Masters*. Like *The Great Divide*, it is based on a historical situation which had occured before Sullivan's experiences in the west, in this case the rivalry for the fur trade between the Hudson's Bay Company and the Northwest Company. Here again Sullivan's experience in similar situations at a later date prepared him to write realistically of the situation. In this novel, as in *The Great Divide*, he is writing historical fiction and not history, but the historical data he uses are accurate. Sullivan's story stresses the exploitation of the Indian by the early fur traders in the west and north of Canada. Neil Campbell emigrates to Canada from Scotland to

11   Alan Sullivan, *With Love From Rachel* (Toronto: Oxford University Press, 1938), p. 13.

work with the Northwest Company; his father had come to the Hudson's Bay Company fifteen years before, and had stopped writing home to his wife. Neil explains why he has come to the Northwest Company:

> The times are hard in Argyle, and while my father's letters did come they did not speak too highly of the service he followed. Also there was nothing for me at home; I consulted with my mother before she died, then sought another part of the new world.[12]

These words could have come from the mouths of many immigrants from Scotland and elsewhere who came to the Canadian west as to a new world in search of a new life. They could also have been spoken by many heroes in early Canadian fiction. They are typical of the attitude of Sullivan heroes: those who take on challenges with courage and confidence. Neil's father, Angus, is embittered by the corruption he has encountered in the dealings of the Hudson's Bay Company with the Indians:

> For the savage once tasting strong drink became undone; it lit fires in his blood, his fortifications tumbled, he was a child pleading for more. . . . Reason grew unhinged; the warrior felt for his ax and was a man to be shunned. For him the world had a sanguinary tinge.[13]

Sullivan justifies the uprisings of the Indians and Metis because of the treatment meted out to them by the fur traders earlier. During one of these uprisings, Neil and Angus meet; Neil saves his father's life.

As in many of his earlier Canadian novels, Sullivan creates vivid descriptions of the settings: York Factory, Montreal in 1800, and the lonely forests to the west of Lake Superior. This gift for description, coupled with his skillful treatment of adventure and suspense and his skillful interweaving of history and fiction, appealed to readers both in Britain and America. For example, the reviewer of *The Fur Masters* for *The Irish Press* of Dublin commented, "Those who like a fine adventurous story will enjoy this book but doubly will they enjoy it if they are interested in the history of the country."[14] The *Inverness Courier* stated that "the whole tale is well constructed, the elements of suspense and

---

12   Alan Sullivan, *The Fur Masters* (London: Murray, 1938), p. 15.
13   Ibid., p. 141.
14   A.J.J., *The Irish Press*, Dublin, May 24, 1938.

surprise are judiciously handled, and the character drawing is of a high standard."[15]

Earlier I have claimed that the environments captured in the paintings of The Group of Seven are frequently the same as those in the writing of Sullivan. I have also quoted John Stevenson's statement that Sullivan had embalmed "in literary form so many great events in the history of the west." *The Fur Masters* is one of the books that clearly illustrates the truth of these two claims and, at the same time, reveals an important difference between the Group of Seven and Sullivan. Where the paintings "embalm" for posterity the primeval environment which may eventually disappear in Canada, Sullivan's writing captures the same environment but places within it the animal and human life which existed there; the visions are filled with movement and sound:

> He spoke with deep feeling, born of years of faithful isolation. In summertime, when nights were short and brigades arrived from the west, life was not so bad. Then when the same brigades were dispatched to inland posts, there followed a liveable season and the penultimate warmth of Indian summer, while the air filled with flights of birds migrating south, swans, geese, and ducks, innumerable flocks whose plump bodies were dried or stored in casks of brine for later consumption. Next the approach of bitter weather, with wind moaning through naked poplars, willows and alder fringing the flat shore. Then winter gripping the land tight, with the great bay frozen for miles out. For those long dark months the post was a bleak spot in which to be marooned with no warm green spruce or hemlock to temper the frigid gales, and Macnab, who limped from an old gunshot wound, found the snowshoe trails too trying for his strength.
>
> . . . .
>
> As always on this occasion the situation was vivacious in the extreme with a babble of excited voices in English and French, broken snatches of song, the maudlin complaints of childlike men, and the strong speech of the agent or commis, who was hard put to assemble his company, many of whom were still sodden with much drink. But beneath the drink and apparent confusion the work of loading went steadily on.
>
> Close at hand floated twenty great canoes—canots du maitre—each thirty-five feet long, sheathed with tawny birchen bark over ribs and laths of white cedar, their seams sewn with fiber

of tough spruce root and sealed with pitch or gum from the same friendly tree. The sharp insolent bows and sterns were boldly fashioned, high-riding, proud, and painted in fantastic colors, while a rib of white ran clear along the gunwale from stem to stern. In the bottom of each had been laid slim straight poles, and on these, to distribute the pressure, were now being laid the five tons of burden.[16]

4

With the Declaration of War in 1939, life changed for most people in the Western world, and the Sullivans were not excluded. The eldest son, D'Arcy, served in the Royal Navy; Barry, the second son, served in the Royal Air Force, Natalie's husband, Quinton Hogg, was also in the service; and, of course, Basil Liddell Hart was a military strategist whose whole life had been spent in the study of wars. When the threat of invasion was a real possibility in 1940, Sheerland House, being in southeastern England was subject to requisition by the army. Alan and Bessie Sullivan returned to Toronto and took up residence at the King Edward Hotel. Although they took trips to Arizona in the winters and to Quebec in the summers, they led a reasonably quiet life during the war. And Sullivan continued to write.

In 1941 Sullivan's third Canadian semi-historical novel, *Three Came to Ville Marie*, was published. It won the Governor General's Award for Fiction in 1941. There is no doubt whatever that Sullivan deserved to win the Governor General's Award; unfortunately, he won it for the wrong book. The awards were first given in 1937, for books published in 1936; this would have disqualified *The Great Divide* but, surely, *The Fur Masters* was a far greater achievement than Gwethalyn Graham's *Swiss Sonata*, which won the award for 1938. Perhaps he was excluded from the competition because he had lived only for the first fifty-two years of his life in Canada. Let us hope that was the reason. Perhaps the committee at the time of *Three Came to Ville Marie* was really making the award on the basis of his earlier novels. In any case, the specific novel chosen for the award is not his best work. When the book was published about two years later in the United States, it received some very polite and some fairly enthusiastic reviews, for example, that by Mary Ross in *The New York Herald Tribune* for

---

16 *The Fur Masters*, pp. 7, 12, 13.

Sunday, January 31, 1943. Of the many American reviews published at the time, one summarizes the plot in brisk strokes—with a freshness perhaps verging on brashness—and provides a fair assessment of the book:

> Laid in the late seventeenth or early eighteenth century, this is historical fiction, Grade B. The three of the title add up to a triangle: Paul who loves Jacqueline, who loves Jules who loves himself. Paul and Jacqueline live in the same town in Britanny. He wants to marry her. When his friend Jules, a dashing musketeer, comes to town, the girl falls in love with him.
>
> Paul and Jules fight a duel. Paul withdraws from the engagement when it has hardly begun. Disgraced, he quits France for Canada. Jules and Jacqueline are married and move to Paris. The lovely bride catches the eye of Louis XIV. A scandal ensues, with the youthful pair going to Canada to escape it. Thus the triangle is reassembled. The perilous life in the wilderness works changes in all three. A battle with the Indians brings the story to a brisk, if easily predictable, climax.
>
> This competently written novel is always on the verge of banality, yet it is slickly presented and never dull. The actual historical figures introduced—and they are numerous—are more than half-alive. Something of the tang of pioneer French Canada is conveyed. The author has his prejudices (the Jesuits, for example), and he rides them hard.[17]

That the novel was welcomed in Canada, Britain, and the United States with a large number of very favourable reviews may be related to the fact that by the time it was published in the United States it was known, as it was headlined by Mary Ross, as "Canada's Prize Novel." That might have called for some diplomacy on the part of American and British reviewers.

In *Three Came to Ville Marie*, against a realistic setting with many historically accurate characterizations, Sullivan presents the story of Paul de Lorimier and Jules and Jacqueline Vicotte. In the relationship of the three characters, three qualities of essential man emerge: loyalty, courage, and a willingness to help others. Although at the beginning of the story the three would seem to have been headed for the situation of the eternal triangle, their superior qualities save them. As in earlier works, Sullivan introduces a strong emphasis on fate: "Fate—destiny—had arranged this—

---

17   Anon. *The Sign*, Union City, New Jersey, February 19, 1943.

they had nothing to do with it—they were puppets—marionettes twitched by invisible strings,—to dance to a new measure on a wild and foreign stage."[18] The story is in the archetypal pattern of Canadian fiction; people leave an old land where life was once happier than at the time of departure and go in search of a new land where happiness is not yet to be realized; they are caught in the cage of the present: "Those who come after us will not know what we have endured, but I pray that on the soil we buy so dearly other generations will live in security and comfort."[19] Those words of Governor Frontenac are typical of the atmosphere that pervades the work.

The presentation of the Governor General's Award took place at a dinner in Montreal; in recognition of the stature of Sullivan there were many distinguished guests present, and it probably gave some satisfaction to Sullivan to be given public recognition at the age of seventy-four in his own country.

During these war years in Canada, Sullivan was active on another front; he was the author of a C.B.C. serial, "Newbridge," which was heard each evening, Monday to Friday, on C.B.C. radio. Newbridge was a thinly disguised Port Hope, a town very familiar to Sullivan. He had, as well, other projects on which he was working. One of these took him on a long trip by rail and air to the Yukon in 1943. What the project was is not known to his family; for our purposes what is important about the trip is that it shows him, at the age of seventy-five, as a very active man, still full of dreams, and with the enthusiasm and vitality to attempt to achieve them. While on the trip, whenever it was at all possible he wrote to his wife Bessie. I have in my files twelve such letters written between November 18 and December 6, 1943. A few selected passages from them reveal his activity and also the warmth of his love for his wife.

On train, November 18th.

Passing through a poor section of this Canada of ours. About all one sees is rabbit tracks in six inches of snow.

Winnipeg, November 19th.

Bless you Old Dutch—you're the girl for me—always.

---

18   Alan Sullivan, *Three Came to Ville Marie* (Toronto: Oxford University Press, 1941), p. 202.
19   Ibid., p. 366.

Winnipeg, November 21th.
The Women's Press Club wanted me for tea Tuesday afternoon.

Winnipeg, November 22nd.
Lunched today with [George] Ferguson of the Free Press. Nice Man. Will see Dafoe on the way back.

Edmonton, November 23rd.
Very lovely sunrise. The Selkirks lying along the western horizon like a ridge of broken egg shells . . . . Bless you sweetheart—you have all my heart—all my love—always—always. I hope for something from you tomorrow.

Edmonton, November 24th.
Hope all goes well with my dearest. Just a week since I started out. Lunched with . . . such a fine fellow, now in charge of the observer's training for the R.C.A.F.

Whitehorse, Yukon Territory, November 26th.
Ever get a letter from the Yukon Territory? No? Well you're getting one now. . . . We are just south of Dawson City in the Klondike District. I had not time to fly in there today as I was "contacting" various local notables—and getting material. . . . Sometimes I observe a not entirely successful effort to conceal surprise at so elderly a person knocking about in what is a young man's country.

Yukon, November 27th.
. . .met some more interesting characters, amongst them a lady sour dough who has lived in this country for 40 years. . . . I wish I were about forty years younger and we had just been married.

Edmonton, November 28th.
I'm really very fit—and reviving my youth in the uncouth north.

Vancouver, November 29th.
Odd to see the mountain tops sticking up through the fog blanket to remind us that there was an earth.

Vancouver, November 30th.
A wire from Winnipeg tells me that the last Patterson freighter sails from Fort William tomorrow but if I wish it they will "canvas the trade" and arrange for my passage later on. I hope about the 10th [of December!].

Winnipeg, December 6th.
Good view of the mountains this time. . . . Today busy with Hudson Bay people. . . . Leave tonight for Fort William and hope

tomorrow to catch a grain freighter. . . . Would you like to spend
next summer in B.C. if we are on this side? There's an interesting
proposition of which I'll tell you. . . . Bless you my dearest love. It
will be joyful to be together again.

Ever devoted,
Alan

In 1944 *And From That Day*, a fictionalized version of the
crucifixion which was dedicated to his mother, was published by
Sullivan. At Easter of that same year, the Toronto Arts and Letters
Club presented his Easter Drama, "The Law and the Prophet,"
directed by Earl Grey. When the war ended in 1945, Alan and
Bessie Sullivan returned to England to live with their daughter,
Mrs. Basil Liddell Hart, at Tilford House, Farnham, Surrey.

In 1946, at the age of seventy-eight, Alan Sullivan saw the
publication of his last book, *Cariboo Road*. The *Montreal Daily Star*
described it as "an excellently written book and Mr. Sullivan has
drawn upon his prowess to make it one of immense interest to every
Canadian."[20] It serves as an excellent farewell appearance for
Sullivan at the end of a long run on the stage of Canadian literature.

Cariboo Road is the story of the adventures of one family—Ma
Bowers, her husband Dan, and their foster daughter Mary—in the
gold rush to the Cariboo district of British Columbia in the early
1860s. The story begins with the Bowers family as they close up
and leave their home on Telegraph Hill, San Francisco, and
describes their adventures on the boat to Seattle, on the Fraser
River, and up the mountain trail from Yale to Richfield. The
events in Richfield are followed through two summers and the
intervening winter.

The plot has three strands: Dan Bowers' search for gold in the
Cariboo; Mary Bowers' choice of a husband between the two rivals,
Harry Harper and Lemuel Flint; the bringing to justice of Dan's
cousin, Stephen Bowers, for his evil deeds. Dan does find gold, and
something of comparable worth; Mary is won by Flint, the gambler, beginning with her first encounters with him and his
ways—good and bad—on the boat from San Francisco, and he in
the process gives up his evil ways. Stephen Bowers, alias Michael

---

20   H.O.H., "Barbering and Gold Rush," a review of *Cariboo Road*, in *The
     Montreal Daily Star*, July 13, 1946.

Trupp, alias James Hollis, of Sacramento, is justly punished before the story ends. Sullivan skillfully manages to weave the three threads of the story together and to keep it moving at a good pace.

The major character in the book, and a tour de force by Sullivan, is the central figure, Ma Bowers. She is established in that position from the first page, where the husband and daughter are looking to her for decisions as they leave their home. She is referred to by her husband as "Mother" or "Ma" or "Mrs. Bowers," indicating the mother-role she fills toward him and everyone else in the story. She mothers the young Harry Harper by adopting him after he falls in the Fraser, buying him clothes and paying his fare on the trail. She mothers the ailing Mrs. Cameron in the last few weeks of terminal illness. When Flint is injured, "she felt like mothering him."[21]

The prayer she prays as she leaves her home reveals that she feels she has "a sort of private partnership" with God;[22] by aligning herself with God, and later with Judge Begbie, she feels herself responsible for the destinies of those she cares about. She sees that Dan needs all the help she will be able to give him if the dream of the Cariboo is not realized. She is concerned about Mary, unprotected in the robust world of men on the journey north and in Richfield, and she wants God to "help Mary get a husband who'll look after her proper."[23] She is described by Dan, towards the end of the book, as "brave, uncomplaining steadfast, smiling when the bitter outweighs the sweet with a faith no misfortune could shake."[24]

Ma Bowers is Sullivan's ideal woman; she is, in addition, a skillful creation of his imagination. It is improbable that she was based on any one person. She was not the type of woman that Sullivan would have known personally, and she is quite unlike his wife or his mother. In Ma Bowers we see illustrated the qualities and characteristics which Sullivan saw as being of the essence of man. She is courageous and loyal, and stoically accepts whatever fate has in store for her. She has that resiliency of character combined with physical strength that is necessary in the struggle for survival in wilderness surroundings. She is possessed of a vision

21 Alan Sullivan, *Cariboo Road* (Toronto: Nelson, 1946), p. 148.
22 Ibid., p. 3.
23 Ibid., p. 31.
24 Ibid., p. 300.

of the future which she is attempting to achieve, but she also has a philosophy which prepares her for the possibility that dreams may not come true and to accept what comes. Perhaps her most outstanding characteristic is that of compassion; her love of her fellow human beings is constantly displayed. As well as creating a woman who combines these attributes, Sullivan presents in Ma Bowers a believable, realistic character. Many will recognize in her a composite figure made up of strong compassionate women seen in real life.

The other major character is Judge Begbie, who is first encountered on the trail. He is "strong in body . . . had a kind face that expressed a kind of Olympian color, and was at the same time the friendliest looking person . . . . He gave [Ma] a sense of relief. . . . and all at once all was as peaceable as possible."[25] He is the confidant of all, and interested in the well-being of all members of the community. He serves as a yardstick of good, sound, human values, and he sees through the outer appearances of those he meets. He perceives the future problems of British Columbia and of Russia in Alaska. He seems to be the embodiment of the good father.

There is a group of characters as well who are "mothered" by Ma Bowers. Ma's husband, Dan, is a man of forty, who will never grow up, and who sees the world with "eyes large and wondering like those of a child."[26] He is so preoccupied with his own concerns that he is oblivious of his wife's reactions and needs. By the conclusion of the book he has learned much of life and of his wife's importance to him.

Mary is torn between Harper and Flint: Harper is a young, ineffectual, affluent Englishman with a superiority complex; Lemuel Flint, a gambler, at first appears to be an evil character and is misjudged by Ma, who thinks he is a philanderer. Lemuel, in fact, was "genuinely attracted to Mary. . . . He was no philanderer, his views about women almost puritanical. . . . There might come the day when he would require a wife, and somehow the disordered tresses of Miss Bowers had given him an unexpected jolt."[27] Gradually, as the story progresses, Lemuel, by his association with

25   Ibid., p. 51.
26   Ibid., p. 72.
27   Ibid., p. 13.

Ma and Mary, and through his experiences in Richfield, experiences a rebirth; he begins to lead a new life.

Throughout his writing, Sullivan demonstrates a talent for effective description. In *Cariboo Road*, there are many fine examples; he was very familiar with the setting of the Rockies and is at home describing that environment. Here is his description of the coming of winter to the Cariboo:

> Winter came to the Cariboo like an old man to a cringing bride: without sound or storm it crept, first a sort of nakedness when one perceived what the earth was made of, then as though this revelation were indecent she drew from the clouds a thin Arctic shroud with which to screen herself. Pools congealed in the tumbled hills, the wild chorus of mountain torrents diminished, the woods were hushed.
>
> Imperceptibly the shroud thickened till the north had no sharp angles left; land and water wedded in stark communion; cariboo and mule deer deserted the land to traverse the lakes, clicking hooves in narrow grooves rutting the powdery plain. The shroud buried a thousand familiar things, proffering nothing in their place; the marks of men's toil were effaced by its nerveless touch; sounds carried far; tall, grey wolves talked to the moon by night on lonely ridges; white-burdened spruce in whose flat frondage yet nestled a suggestion of warmth flung blue shadows on unwrinkled drifts; ivory-beaked ravens explored the silence on ragged wings.[28]

At times, the description takes on symbolic meaning through the use of concrete images. "Spring came to the Cariboo like a smiling gaoler with jangling keys,"[29] is both a dramatic opening for a chapter and imagery rich in symbolism.

Sullivan's view of life in this novel, as in his earlier works, is usually expressed indirectly, through the thoughts and words of his characters. There is, however, one place where the author directly comes on stage, in what may be considered by some to be author intrusion:

> It takes several kinds of people to make a country:—First, the restless folk who can't stay put; they want to start out, it doesn't much matter where, but somewhere, almost always west or north; it may be the sheriff is after them, or for some other reason they themselves don't understand—they just don't care so long as they

28 Ibid., p. 191.
29 Ibid., p. 231.

do start. They seldom leave any trail or tracks to speak of, perhaps a few blazes here and there in timber land, or black patches from camp fires, or a tin kettle with a hole in it—but not much more. Anyway they get somewhere, that's the main thing. They are just born rovers, feet shod with quicksilver. These are the trail seekers.

Later someone hears of something good, it may be out west, and more people start: these do leave a sort of path you can follow; here and there a big tree felled across a creek, or a blaze with pencilled information for the next comer, or a cleft stick with a note 'good water one half mile north', or a hewn cross with name and date, or something like that. Often they change their minds, taking a fancy to some spot on the way, and hunt and trap and make friends with the natives if there are any. In winter they live in thick bush in hunting lodges, in summer on a lake or stream where the flies aren't too bad. These are the trail makers.

The third lot is again different; it moves slowly, turning paths into dirt roads, opening short cuts; it builds trading posts and log bridges and timber landings for boats and canoes on the waterways; it blasts big boulders, burns stumps, and doesn't want to get anywhere in particular itself, but wants the road to get there. These are the roads makers.

The next still again different, mostly older some quite old, not so interested in gold as to find soil instead of the worn out land at home: they bring families and all you can get into a wagon, and all beasts that can walk behind a wagon, and a dog. When you bring a dog it means something. Crossing new unbroken land for the first time, they travel slowly, halting now and then to turn over the soil, squeeze a fistful, crumble and smell it, looking this way and that for water and drainage and grazing, timber for fuel and building and fencing.

At last when the right place is found, and before he does anything else, the man will unload his plough, and hitch up a pair of horses or oxen to turn the first furrow and see how the land feels against the share, while his women and children stand by, saying nothing, but somehow sure that something wonderful is going on. They are quite right in this, for when a man drives the point of a plough into new soil in a new country he is doing something wonderful, and hitching himself to what is deep, precious and eternal, for this is what finally shapes a country, and will endure long after the last prospector has washed the last ounce of gold from the last creek in the district. These are the home makers.

And all these people are necessary to each other.[30]

---

30   Ibid., pp. 226-27.

This intrusion by Sullivan into the story is possibly justified by his use of the analogy in the passage which is related to the title of the chapter, "On The Making of Roads." At the end of a long life, much of it spent breaking ground as a prospector and explorer, Sullivan has given us, in a concrete way, the history of the Canadian pioneering experience. Anyone who has read, either in history or fiction, of the early settlement of Canada cannot but recognize in this excerpt a vivid capturing of the human condition of those who made our country.

Many of the typical characteristics of Canadian fiction appear in this novel. It is concerned with a search for identity—by Ma Bowers, by Flint, and by Dan. It is a search for a new paradise, be it El Dorado or the Garden of Eden. There is in the search the aspect of regeneration, as in the case of Flint. Survival on the new venture is the concern of Ma Bowers. The characters all experience isolation, in various situations, whether it is in the boat, on the trail, or in Richfield. Any one of these locations could be seen as a "garrison" or a cage. In Richfield during the winter, "the people felt very small; they were so much smaller than the bigness around them . . . people cling together to share each other's life warmth."[31] The imagery of the dream recurs throughout the novel, dreams of the past and of the future—"they all had their dreams."[32] Ma's dream of the past was Telegraph Hill; for the future it was of cattle raising in the Cariboo, "a real home, and good land, where [she'd] have a garden."[33] Surely, the Garden of Eden of the future! These are personal dreams, but the responsible citizen, Judge Begbie, has national dreams, "dreams of this western land."[34]

Superficially, the novel concerns the Bowers' search for gold in the Cariboo in the 1860s, but the story can also be interpreted as the journey, or search, on the part of humanity for the treasure, or meaning, of life. In Sullivan's view, life is enduring with hope; life itself is the quest. "It wasn't the possession of gold they found their joy in, but the pursuit of it. All they asked was sweat, and labour, and hunger and toil and the bright promise at the end of the

---

31   Ibid., p. 204.
32   Ibid., p. 209.
33   Ibid., p. 155.
34   Ibid., p. 276.

trail."[35] This last novel is, in a way, a "summing up" of Sullivan's view of human life. It is an excellent conclusion to his long life.

6

During the early months of 1947 Sullivan thought that he would feel better if he were to get some sun; he and his wife went to Marrakech, French Morocco. Early in the summer, on his way back to England, he became ill at Monte Carlo. During his illness he underwent surgery with only a local anaesthetic; when the doctor came to see him after the operation, he said to Barry Sullivan and his sister that "this man is the most courageous I have ever met in the face of pain. When we had finished operating on him for nearly two hours, and he was conscious all the time he said 'Sit down sir, you must be very tired.' It was incredible."[36]

Earlier in 1947, Sullivan's translation into English of a Canadian novel written in French, *Boss of the River*, by Félix-Antoine Savard, was published. In Sullivan's foreword to the novel he wrote the following:

> It is hoped that this story may do something to indicate what a wealth of artistic creative treasure is to be found in the work of other French-Canadian writers that has as yet had no English interpretation . . . and thus advance the cause of Canadian unity.[37]

At the close of his life Sullivan was still working towards Canadian unity and understanding. This had been a life-long crusade.

A few days before his death, Sullivan asked his son Barry to have him taken back to England. Barry personally flew the chartered aircraft. Alan Sullivan died on August 6, in his seventy-ninth year, at Tilford House, the home of Basil and Kathleen Liddell Hart in Surrey. The funeral service was held in the Tilford Parish Church, and by Sullivan's request, his body was cremated. John Stevenson, a few weeks later, wrote about Sullivan:

> The friends of Alan Sullivan will keep green to the end of their own lives the memory of a warm hearted man of high character and ability, whose fine sensitive mind and notable gifts as a witty talker

---

35 Ibid., p. 84.
36 Barry Sullivan, notes written during the summer of 1947 in Monte Carlo (in author's files).
37 Alan Sullivan, Foreword to Félix-Antoine Savard, *Boss of the River*, translated by Alan Sullivan (Toronto: Ryerson, 1947), p. vii.

and raconteur made him a delightful companion. Some time before his death he told one of his sons that "he wanted to die with [his] back to a tree in the Canadian woods." but it was not to be. Yet, even if his ashes repose in the little churchyard of Tilford in the countryside of highly civilized Surrey, his spirit will surely find its way back to haunt the wild woodlands of Canada which he knew and loved so well.[38]

---

38 John A. Stevenson, "Alan Sullivan, Poet, Engineer," *Saturday Night* 62 (August 23, 1947), p. 25.

VI

The Summing Up

Alan Sullivan rarely wrote about his creative talent, but in 1929, the same year in which Grove's *It Needs To Be Said* appeared, he published an article, previously mentioned in this work, in which he set out, in typical Sullivan down-to-earth manner, his theory about the writing of fiction. A good place to start in assessing a writer's literary contribution is his own evaluation of what it was he was attempting to accomplish. The relevant part of his comments follows:

> In spite of the difficulty of expressing rational views concerning one's own work, there do seem to be certain conclusions shared by other writers whose life has afforded them the change of scene and occupation I found in my own. One of these is that all actual work of any kind and in any place turns out to be of subsequent value to the writer. It has been my good fortune to travel a great deal and to do, or attempt to do, a great many different things, and it has all borne some kind of literary fruit. . . .
>
> A further conclusion is that the construction of a work of fiction has very little of what one might call system. To put this in another way, you may either first of all visualize certain characters and leave it to them, if they are sufficiently alive, to do certain things which ultimately will form themselves into some sort of plot or situation. If your characters, thus brought into vivid life in your imagination, are real and veritable it is impossible for them to remain inactive. You will find them doing certain things, saying certain other things, and gradually out of all these they will arrange themselves in some relation to each other with individual ambi-

tions, dislikes, points of view, tendencies and characteristics, and there in a rough sort of way is the general scope of your story. Or, if you desire, you may do the contrary. First, you may conceive a certain situation, a certain sequence of events and the resultant finale which constitutes your climax. This done, and what you might call the run of the thing clear in your mind, you may create the various personages necessary consistently to fill the various parts.

To this I will add one thing more; which is that if your characters are really alive, if your imagination has fixed in them certain qualities and tendencies and points of view, you will discover every now and then that they will get up on their hind legs and flatly refuse to do something that you had intended they should do. There is nothing wrong about this. On the contrary, it is an excellent sign, because it means when this happens that you have in your mind created something which is very lifelike and consequently declines to perform what for him or her would be an unnatural act.[1]

Although Sullivan writes in the language of a layman, while Grove adopts the style of the literary critic, I see several parallels in Grove's theory as outlined in the preface of this work and Sullivan's view of fiction as expressed in the excerpt quoted above. Grove's emphasis on the artist as the "indispensable medium" who expresses the "response to what is not I" is surely much the same as Sullivan's statement about the influence of his travels on his own writing. Another view common to them both concerns characterization. Sullivan's statement about his characters getting "up on their hind legs and flatly refus[ing]" to act as the author intended has the same implication as Grove's statement about Abe Spalding, the major character in his *Fruits of the Earth*:

> I lived my life, he his. As I grew older, he did, slowly maturing, slowly changing, slowly shaping his life as best he could. We were never one; although I felt with him we remained two; I had suffered too intensely from his nature to identify myself with him at any time.[2]

I believe that Sullivan's comment about characterization is closely related to what Ethel Wilson meant when she wrote that

---

1 Alan Sullivan, "In the Matter of Alan Sullivan," *Ontario Library Review* 14 (November 1929), 36.
2 Frederick Philip Grove, *In Search of Myself* (Toronto: Macmillan, 1946), p. 261.

"the very best writing in our country will result from an incandescence which takes place in a prepared mind where forces meet."

Sullivan's remarks about the way in which personal experiences bear literary fruit are quite similar to remarks made by such Canadian writers as Sinclair Ross, Margaret Laurence, and Hugh MacLennan which stress the importance of a "sense of place" in creating successful fiction. Although the Canadian setting has been emphasized in this work with regard to Sullivan, it has to be remembered that he did have extensive knowledge of, and experience in, several parts of Europe and North Africa. His life in England, for example, made it possible for him to write with ease about English settings and English life. The same is true of Mediterranean areas. If Sullivan's remarks are taken quite literally, they are valid; one has only to place the history of Sullivan's life alongside his publications, and the parallels are obvious. Almost without exception, his writing reflects incidents he had experienced earlier, settings in which he had lived, and in some cases, people whom he had known. Sullivan's wide spectrum of experience was probably the greatest single factor contributing to his success as a writer. The following passage from Sullivan's story "In Portofino" could only have been written by one who had lived there:

> He seemed, coming towards me through the olive grove, to have detached himself from it, so perfectly did the grey-green of him blend with the twisted roots and narrow, faintly shimmering curtain overhead, an old man, gnarled and bent, with something of the unexpected angularity of the trees around him, dark eyes that retained an active lustre, broad, stooping shoulders, and knotted fingers. He carried a pannier of cones from the slopes above, where olive yields to pine, and the pine dwindles as it climbs the naked sun-smitten heights that march magnificently along the Ligurian coast. He was taking the cones to Portofino, three kilometres away.
>
> "Buon giorno," I said. "Fa bello temp."
>
> He sat down, the basket still on his back, and one could almost hear his bones creak like the dry wicker.
>
> "The weather, yes, it is good." he answered with a grave smile; "but this tramontane wind, it does not promise well. Look!"
>
> His English surprised me, but I looked. The tops of the hills behind Chiaveri were obscured their summits melting vaguely into hanging clouds. But it was the best day we had had for a week.

"You have travelled," I ventured.

He nodded. "Yes, but one comes back."

I could understand that, never having found a spot so serene, so welcoming, as this God-given refuge, to which I had only that day returned, Portofino, and what went with Portofino was a sheer gem. I had lived there previously for months above the Ristorante Nazionale, where Catina, her hair in a tight knot, brought in the bath water and opened the shutters to let in the morning sun; where Lena Razzolo made delectable things in a kitchen that would have delighted Arthur Rackham; and Alessandro, her brother, drove the two unimpressionable white horses that pulled the diligence to Santa Margherita, and modern hotels with central heat and the Italian luxury tax.[3]

In Sullivan's discussion of "the construction of a work of fiction," the first alternative mentioned by him, that of starting with characters and letting them "form themselves into some sort of plot or situation," is a technique used very successfully by him, although it must be noted that in books like *The Great Divide* or *The Fur Masters* the historical framework of the stories was ready-made. His ability to create realistic, powerful characters, without ponderous descriptive passages to introduce them, is one of Sullivan's greatest skills.

In *The Passing of Oul-I-But and Other Tales*, Tom Moore, the laconic, honest half-breed, who remains so loyal to the company he serves, emerges from the page to remain with the reader for a lifetime. In the same book, Na-Quape, the majestic Indian Chief, captures the greatness that lived in Indian leaders like Big Bear, of whom Rudy Wiebe has written so effectively. Brian Blantyre, in *Blantyre—Alien*, is dramatically presented as the man with such integrity that he sacrifices his life for his wife's happiness. In *The Inner Door*, Kenneth Landon is clearly the controlling figure in the novel: he is a perfect example of what Sullivan means when he says that "you will find them doing certain things." Landon, the man from the establishment who becomes a labour leader, is probably a "Walter Mitty" projection of Sullivan himself. In his writings it often becomes obvious that Sullivan, in his own philosophy of life, opposed the motives of the rich and powerful, although, paradoxically, he was drawn in their direction in his personal life.

---

3 Alan Sullivan, "In Portofino," in E. J. O'Brien (ed.), *Best Short Stories 1927*, Vol. 12 (Boston: Houghton Mifflin, 1928), p. 280.

Robert Fisher Clark, in *The Rapids*, was completely patterned after Francis H. Clergue; and Sullivan, in his presentation of the man, has captured so much of the real Clergue that Clark emerges as a brilliant piece of characterization. In "The passing of Chantie, the Curlew" (in *Under the Northern Lights*), Chantie, an old woman, arouses great sympathy when she brings about her own death as a result of her struggle to kill the Polar Bear in order to sustain life for her family. She is one of several Indian and Eskimo characters in Sullivan's writings who may have been drawn from people he had met in his travels in the West and North of Canada. Regardless of where the inspiration came from, the characters are quickly and skillfully drawn, and remain memorable. In the case of John Caxton, the hero of *In The Beginning*, the philosophical concepts of this anthropologist emerge so naturally in his conversations with his daughter and her two suitors that the reader can imagine Caxton sitting across from him in his comfortable study.

Like Clark, Jock Mactier, the retired Royal Canadian Mounted Police sergeant in *The Magic Makers*, could quite possibly be patterned on a real person, a member of the force. Mactier, in his search for the missing Scotsman in the Arctic, arouses the admiration of the reader, who can picture him involved in incidents other than those in this specific novel. Big John Hickey, in *The Great Divide*, could be a composite of the railroad workers whom Sullivan knew when working for the C.P.R. Rachel Bedell in *With Love from Rachel*, on the other hand, is completely a creation of Sullivan's imagination, and a brilliant one! Neil Campbell is both highly individualized and also the archetypal Scottish immigrant to Western Canada. Ma Bowers, of *Cariboo Road*, as has been suggested earlier, may quite well be Sullivan's masterpiece of characterization.

It is well to point out that Sullivan's skill in characterization accounts for his success with short stories. Although they are given superficial treatment in this work, they are of major importance in any literary evaluation of the author. The majority of his successful short stories, among the hundreds published, are those in which a central character is presented in a setting and a situation which reveal the character quickly and effectively.

The second alternative presented by Sullivan as a technique in the construction of fiction—beginning first with plot and then creating characters "to fill the various parts"—is placed in the correct order with regard to his own writing. When Sullivan resorted to the latter method, he was rarely successful. Many of the books in the prolific period 1929-1934 put plot first and characterization second. The result is what one would expect: melodramatic treatment of situations, with a sacrifice of realism and richness of characterization. Although Sullivan was not an innovator in plot construction, he was successful in writing some novels and short stories that depended on plot rather than on characterization for their effects. *The Jade God* is a good example; most of the appeal of this book, and of the play based on it, depends on suspense, mystery, and adventure. In *The Jade God*, as in much of his writing, Sullivan proves that he is a master of dialogue. In his fiction, whether it stresses characterization or plot, Sullivan always succeeds in writing realistic and effective dialogue, which is one of his major assets in revealing and developing character. In analysis of fiction, or any other creative writing, the danger is that a simplistic approach can distort the author's work. Therefore, it must be interjected here that a nice distinction cannot always be drawn between works which emphasize character and those emphasizing plot; in the same way, one cannot ignore other aspects of a writer's ability. Without Sullivan's skill with dialogue, many of his strong characters might never have emerged. Without at least some excellent characterization in his novels of suspense and mystery, the books would not have been published. Sullivan's effective use of dialogue certainly made it easy to change *The Jade God* from a novel to a play and *The Great Divide* from a novel to a movie script. His dialogue added a dramatic dimension to all of his writing. As with the writing of Robertson Davies at the present time, Sullivan's fiction lends itself to television, radio, stage, and screen adaptations. Sullivan, of course, came before the era of television, but several of his works were adapted for the earlier medium, radio.

Towards the end of Sullivan's article about his own writing he makes brief comments about theme and style:

> Another conclusion is, and I submit it in all consideration to all Canadian writers who are fortunate in being considerably younger than myself, that one must guard against the temptation to over elaborate one's theme. It is very easy to drown a story in words. . . .
> Thus in later years there has been evolved a modern school of fiction which though making no pretence at literary grace, gives neverthe-

less a remarkably exact representation of life as lived by the men
and women of today. This is the obverse of the later Victorian two
volume novel, which generally was weighed down with stilted and
self-conscious attempts at literary style.

I am not qualified to give advice to anyone, but do suggest to
our younger Canadian writers that the stuff of the story is the first
consideration and that, lacking the stuff, no literary gymnastics
will make up the obvious shortage.[4]

Sullivan has certainly followed his own advice with regard to the
first element, theme. Although basic themes emerge in Sullivan,
expecially in his best writing, he does not come on stage to preach
about them; in this respect he is, again, in accord with the theory
of Grove. One cannot miss Sullivan's emphasis on the theme of
survival, but the thematic development emerges from the characters, the plot, and the atmosphere, rather than being explicitly
mentioned. *Brother Eskimo* is a story of survival; Keleepeles and his
young brother, Cunayou, are deliberately left on their own to see if
they can survive. John Caxton, in *In The Beginning*, takes Gregory
Burden and Philip Sylvester to Patagonia to see if they can survive.
But in neither of these books does Alan Sullivan appear to point us
to his theme. In the same way, Sullivan develops his belief in the
stoical acceptance of death; at no time in his writing is there any
obsession with death; it is always presented in a matter-of-fact
way. This treatment of death, combined with specific examples of
characters who speak of accepting death, makes quite clear to the
reader what Sullivan wants him to understand. The Canadian
theme of the vision, or dream, of the future is obvious in Sullivan's
writing; *The Great Divide*, the story of Canada's national dream,
immediately comes to mind.

When one looks at the complete works of Sullivan, it becomes clear that his major theme is the essence of Man, the
elemental characteristics which together produce an ideal man.
But, when one looks at an individual novel or story one is not
overwhelmed by this thematic concern. Neil Campbell of *The Fur
Masters*, or Jock Mactier in *The Magic Makers*, obviously are
versions of Sullivan's ideal man, as is Clark in *The Rapids* or Judge
Begbie in *Cariboo Road*. At no time in these books is there a
strident introduction of any of them as such an ideal.

4   Alan Sullivan, "In the Matter of Alan Sullivan," p. 36.

Before proceeding to the last element of fiction discussed by Sullivan, that of style, this attempt to analyze his writing in general terms should consider a question closely related to theme: What, if anything, makes Sullivan a distinctly Canadian writer? The answer must be based largely on theme and content. There is nothing in his technical treatment of plot or of characterization that could be related to any particular Canadian trait. But in both theme and content—which here includes setting—there are distinctive Canadian characteristics.

Sullivan's constant references to isolation, the struggle for survival, and the dreams or visions of the characters are Canadian characteristics. This is not to suggest that these elements do not exist in non-Canadian writing, but that the constant use of them is a characteristic of Canadian literature, in general, and of Sullivan's writings in particular. In addition, they show a concern for the Canadian identity. Sullivan's particular contribution in this typically Canadian concern is the link he makes between the search for a Canadian identity as a nation and the search of individual characters for the essence of Man. These two quests come together, as has been mentioned, in Big John Hickey and to some extent in his whole cavalcade of Canadian characters.

The content of most of Sullivan's successful fiction is Canadian; some of it is exclusively Canadian. The content of the three books of short stories and sketches, *The Passing of Oul-I-But*, *Under the Northern Lights*, and *The Cycle of the North*, is all peculiar to the Canadian west and north. None of it could possibly belong in the literature of another country. The same is true of his major novels: *The Great Divide*, *The Fur Masters*, and *Cariboo Road*. Novels such as *The Rapids* and *Brother Eskimo* are also exclusively Canadian in content. Even some of the Sinclair Murray works are Canadian, for example, *With Love From Rachel* and *The Golden Foundling*. As to setting, there is little that needs to be said; descriptions of Canada pervade his writing—the Rockies, the forests of north-western Ontario, the Arctic, Hudson's Bay, the Laurentians, the St. Lawrence River, and so forth. If Sullivan had only managed to write about the Maritimes, he could have been the most representative of all Canadian writers in use of settings. Shortly before his death he expressed regret that in his travels he had missed one part of Canada completely—Labrador. Not only are the settings in much of his writing uniquely Canadian, but the descriptions of them are superb. A number of them have already been quoted. Here is another from "The Passing of Chantie, The Curlew":

> The North is a stern mother to the tribes that tenant her silent places. She feeds them for a time, then, perchance, starves them. She bakes them under a torrid sun and in a little while, strikes them with killing winds. She smiles across leagues of sunny waters that soon are hidden beneath endless fields of grinding ice. She dangles her purple Aurora in the zenith that all may see the marvel, but out of her unknown regions come roaring the storms that no man may face and live. So beneath her threats and caresses the brown people are what they are: brave, simple and uncomplaining; wistful, because they know not when the end may come; loving the slant-eyed children for whose safety they are ready to die; generous, because hunger is brother to all, and, when old age comes, facing the final great adventure with unquestioning fortitude and faith.[5]

An important aspect of style, the last matter discussed by Sullivan in his article, and also related to settings, is his use of symbolism. Sullivan frequently uses concrete images to symbolize ideas and ideals. Some of these symbols are borrowed from his own life; some are creations of his fertile imagination. Some are, in fact, characters used symbolically. Such characters, like those in Conrad, are embodiments of an ideal. This can lead to "larger than life" figures, but it is an accepted technique. Conrad's Lord Jim is both a person and a symbol; Sullivan's Robert Fisher Clark is also both. In much the same way Sullivan makes use of houses: many are realistically described and closely resemble houses in which Sullivan lived, but some of them, like that of Abe Spalding in Frederick Philip Grove's *Fruits of the Earth*, take on a halo of symbolic meaning. Whispering Lodge is both Sheerland House and a symbol of the English way of life. It also contributes to the mysterious atmosphere of the novel. The Bishop's home in *The Rapids* is actually Bishophurst in Sault Ste. Marie, but it is also symbolic of the "establishment" of the small town. Rachel's hut is realistically described as a home in Aklavik, but it is used, as well, to symbolize the values held by this remarkable woman. The statue in *What Fools Men Are* could be a statue in the central square of any Mediterranean city; it is also symbolic of the vanity of men and

---

5 Alan Sullivan, "The Passing of Chantie, The Curlew," in *Under the Northern Lights* (London: Dent, 1926), p. 146.

nations that leads to war. The piece of soft tanned hide sent to Edinburgh from the Arctic is a realistic concrete item in *The Magic Makers*; it is also a concrete symbol of the resourcefulness of Henry Rintoul in his struggle for survival.

The Indian pipe that appears in various Sullivan pieces is another example of effective use of symbol. In *The White Canoe and Other Verse*, Sullivan's first published work, one poem is entitled "To My Pipe" and another "To My Indian Pipe." In *Venice and Other Poems*, written two years later, he again included a poem with the title "To My Pipe." In the story "The Defiance of Na-quape," in his first published book of fiction, *The Passing of Oul-I-But and Other Tales*, Sullivan writes of the peace pipe with its yard-long stem which Na-quape passes around the circle which included the inexperienced envoy, Blantyre:

> The pipe was very old, and without question, very dirty; and Blantyre's lips that clung so tenaciously to his brier, lifted instinctively. He could not guess that he was asked to share in a ceremonial that was pregnant with meaning to every red man. He only knew that the thing was to him unspeakably filthy, and, just as he was about to imperil the life of every white settler in the country, the Sergeant whispered: "Take it, sir, for God's sake take it!" So the deputy took it and drew a whiff of acrid smoke, while tense sinews relaxed and invisible short guns were laid softly down beneath draped blankets by the silent semicircle on the grass.
>
> . . . .
>
> As Blantyre listened, he became slowly aware that he was reading one of the mysteries of the world, for, far back as nations go, no one of them but can trace its parentage to some ancient stock, while this wild man, who talked so proudly, seemed to be sprung, indeed from the wild land he trod. There was a fibre in the blue-eyed Englishman that answered to this; and as he listened he learned, till out of his learning began to grow that respect shared by all who knew the red man as he was before he became what his white brother made him. Blantyre had heard orators, but he had never before recognized the truth as he got it from Na-quape. The chief held out the pipe again: "It is the pipe of Peguis, the Chief of Chiefs," he said simply and this time it did not seem so dirty to Blantyre.[6]

---

6 Alan Sullivan, *The Passing of Oul-I-But and Other Tales* (Toronto: J. M. Dent, 1913), pp. 260-67.

Sullivan smoked a pipe during much of his life; he also became
familiar very early with the symbolic significance of the Indian
pipe. The whole plot of this short story, and the revelation of
character of both Na-quape and Blantyre, depend on the one
concrete image of the Indian pipe. It is an excellent example of the
symbolic use to which Sullivan puts concrete images. The pipe is
an actual physical object that takes on a halo of symbolic meaning,
which develops Sullivan's theme better than would be possible by
any piece of explanatory writing. Many other examples of Sullivan's imaginative use of major symbols could be cited: in the titles
of the two novels *The Crucible* and *The Jade God* two symbols are
introduced. The first one has already been mentioned; the second
refers to a jade figurine which symbolizes the supernatural atmosphere created in the story.

Reference has already been made to John Stevenson's statement about Sullivan's "service to Canada to embalm . . . great
events . . . and famous characters."[7] One of the finest examples of
this is the end of *The Rapids*, first in the description of Clark's
return to St. Mary's as witnessed by his engineer, Belding, and
Belding's wife Elsie, and then in the "Conclusion," which is an
epilogue to the story of Clergue-Clark and an example of a character treated both as person and symbol:

> Clark was absolutely motionless. . . . The train moved on, till it
> halted for a few moments on the great bridge. The air was cool and
> full of the deep roar of the rapids, and the car vibrated delicately
> with the huge steel girders on which it rested. Two hundred feet
> away came the first, smooth dip that Belding would always re-
> member. Immediately beneath, he had slid into the chaos further
> on.
>
> The two young people did not stir, but watched the silent
> observer. Against the window they caught the dominant nose, the
> clean cut, powerful chin, the aggressive contour of head and
> shoulders. Clark was leaning forward, his gaze exploring the well
> remembered scene.
>
> "Don't disturb him," whispered Elsie again.
>
> Her husband pressed her hand, and they waited, wondering
> what thoughts were passing through that marvelous brain. He was
> staring at the works. It was all his—this dream come true; this

---

7   John A. Stevenson, "Alan Sullivan, Poet, Engineer," *Saturday Night* 62
    (August 23, 1947), 25.

vision portrayed in steel and stone. Out of nothing but water and wood and his own superb faith he had created it, only to see this exemplification of himself slip from his own hands into those of others, who had sponsored neither its birth nor its magnificent development. What portion of his leader, pondered the engineer, had been incorporated in those vast foundations—and what had life left in store to replace them for him?

. . . .

The sumac leaves, which through the summer months tapped delicately at my study window, have turned a vivid scarlet, and one by one have fluttered to the ground. Here, by the mysterious process of nature, they will be incorporated with the rich soil, to nourish some other life that will later climb sunward. But in that life no one shall recognize a sumac leaf.

So it seems are the efforts of men. A few years of growth and aspiration—then the fiery bourgeoning to a climax, and, after that, incorporation in the soil of a forgetfulness that seems indifferent alike to their exertions and their ambitions. But the end is not here. Somewhere, and most certainly in some other form, the effort achieves immortality and reasserts itself, indestructible and eternal. For such are the myriad filaments of existence, and so indissolubly are men linked with each other by invisible chains, that it is but seldom that impulse can be traced back to its birth, or courage to its starting point.

Who then shall determine what is success and what is failure? Does the grandeur of the reward establish the value of the service, or is it not true that, in the mysterious cycle of time, the richest field is not seldom sown by hands that have been without honor or recognition in their season? Does wealth or authority spell success, or is it the meed of those who have given rather than taken, who have toiled on the mountain side rather than sought the peaks of publicity? Clark came to St. Mary's a poor man, and he left it no whit the richer. What he made, he spent. And when the day of his departure dawned, he went as one who had attempted and failed, carrying with him the resentment of those who lost, and few thanks from those who profited.

But did Clark actually fail?

To-day the mines of Algoma are supplying steel rails for Asiatic railways; the forests about St. Marys are yielding pulp for Australia, and the great power house is sending carbide to the mines of India. This and much more is the fruit of vision. What matter that Philadelphia stormed, and that the reins of government were snatched from those masterful hands? The dream has come true.

Consider for a moment this man, who is stranger to most. He desired neither wealth nor ease, being filled with a vast hunger for creation, and to forest, mountain and river he turned with confidence and abiding courage. It was as though nature herself had whispered misty secrets in his ear. Being a prophet, he suffered like a prophet, but the years, rolling on, have enabled him to look back on the later flower of his earlier days, for it was written that he should plow and others reap. And of necessity it was so. Like the prospector who finds gold in the wilderness and straightway shoulders his pack to seek for further treasure, his unwearying soul drove him on in steadfast pursuit of that which lay just over the hill. It was not the thing that lay at his feet which fascinated, but the promise of the morrow, whose dawn already gilded the horizon of his spirit.

Clark, with his impetuous energy, is typical of a country in which few achievements are impossible. He provided his own motive power and used his hypnotic influence only in one direction—that of progress. Ever faithful to his destiny, he was too busy to have time to suffer, too occupied to waste himself in regrets. Like the rapids themselves, his work moves on, and in its deep rumble may be distinguished the confused note of humanity, striving and ever striving.[8]

With a few changes, this passage written by Sullivan about Francis Clergue could serve as Sullivan's own epitaph. Although Clergue's accomplishments were in the field of industry and finance, and Sullivan will be remembered primarily for his achievements in the field of literature, the driving force within the two men was similar. Although Clergue was an American and Sullivan was in so many ways British, both can be viewed as symbolic of Canada itself—of its drive to achieve its destiny, of its attempt to realize its dream. Sullivan has described Clergue as a prophet, by which he means a man with a vision; Sullivan too, can be seen in the same light. His dream had many facets. Some of these relate to a national dream. Sullivan, as an explorer and engineer, was attempting to realize the physical aspects of the national dream. As a novelist, he wrote of that dream and captured for us some of the exciting episodes in the quest for its realization. *The Great Divide* vividly dramatizes the political and financial miracle of uniting Canada physically by building the Canadian Pacific Railway. *The*

---

8 Alan Sullivan, *The Rapids* (Toronto: Copp Clark, 1920), pp. 333-37.

Fur Masters concerns the struggle during an earlier period, when Canadian unity was in danger. *Cariboo Road* tells of the joys and sorrows of those who followed that road in search of material wealth. In these three novels there is always present the atmosphere of vitality and confidence which was an essential part of those three periods in the history of the growth of Canada toward nationhood. If one wishes to assess the contribution of Sullivan to Canadian literature, it is in his books that the answer will be found; in much of what he has written, one will find not only the essence of Man, but some of the essence of Canada.

Bibliography

Works by Alan Sullivan

Verse

The White Canoe and Other Verse. Toronto: J. E. Bryant Co., 1891. Pp. 30.
Venice and Other Verse. Toronto: J. E. Bryant Co., 1893. Pp. 48.

Sayings

I Believe That_____. Toronto: Wm. Tyrell and Co. Pp. 59

Collections of Short Stories[1]

The Cycle of the North. London: J. M. Dent, 1938. Pp. 108.
The Passing of Oul-I-But and Other Tales. Toronto: J. M. Dent, 1913. Pp. 302.
Under the Northern Lights. London: J. M. Dent, 1926. Pp. 218.

History

Aviation in Canada: 1917-1918. Toronto: Rous and Mann, 1919. Pp. 318.

Novels

A Little Way Ahead. Toronto: Macmillan, 1930. Pp. 316.
"And From That Day." Toronto: Ryerson, 1944. Pp. 195.
Antidote. By Sinclair Murray (pseud.). London: J. Murray, 1932. Pp. 332.
Blantyre—Alien. London: J. M. Dent, 1914. Pp. 265.

---

1 No attempt has been made to list Sullivan's short stories that are not included in these three collections.

Brother Blackfoot. New York: Century, 1927. Pp. 300.

Brother Eskimo. Toronto: McClelland and Stewart, 1921. Pp. 249.

Cariboo Road. Toronto: Nelson, 1946. Pp. 311.

Colonel Pluckett. London: Ward Lock, 1932. Pp. 256.

Cornish Interlude. By Sinclair Murray (pseud.). London: J. Murray, 1932. Pp. 303.

Double Lives. By Sinclair Murray (pseud.). Toronto: Macmillan, 1929. Pp. 318.

Golden Foundling. By Sinclair Murray (pseud.). Toronto: Macmillan, 1931. Pp. 318.

Human Clay. By Sinclair Murray (pseud.) and B. V. Shann. London: J. Murray, 1926. Pp. 318.

In the Beginning. London: Hurst & Blackett, 1926. Pp. 280.

John Frensham, K. C. By Sinclair Murray (pseud.) and B. V. Shann. London: J. Murray, 1925. Pp. 320.

Man at Lone Tree. London: Ward Lock, 1933. Pp. 256.

Mr. Absalom. London: Murray, 1930. Pp. 316.

No Secrets Island. London: Murray, 1931. Pp. 314.

Queer Partners. By Sinclair Murray (pseud.). Toronto: Macmillan, 1930. Pp. 318.

The Birthmark. London: Arnold, 1924. Pp. 319.

The Broken Marriage. By Sinclair Murray (pseud.). New York:Dutton, 1929. Pp. 319.

The Crucible. By Sinclair Murray (pseud.). London: Bles, 1925. Pp. 318.

The Days of Their Youth. New York: Century, 1926. Pp. 332.

The Fur Masters. London: Murray, 1938. Pp. 320.

The Great Divide: A Romance of The Canadian Pacific Railway. London: Lovat Dickson and Thompson, 1935. Pp. 417.

The Inner Door. Toronto: Gundy, 1917. Pp. 388.

The Ironmaster. London: J. Murray, 1931. Pp. 345.

The Jade God. Toronto: F. D. Goodchild, 1925. Pp. 312. Dramatized as a three-act play, with the same title, in collaboration with William Edwin Barry. New York: French, 1930. Pp. 77.

The Magic Makers. London: J. Murray, 1930. Pp. 297.

The Money Spinners. By Sinclair Murray (pseud.). London: Low Martson, 1936. Pp. 378.

The Obstinate Virgin. London: Low Marston, 1934. Pp. 314.

The Rapids. Toronto: Copp Clark, 1920. Pp. 337.

The Splendid Silence. New York: Dutton, 1927. Pp. 278.

The Story of One-Ear. London: George Philip and Son, 1929. Pp. 68.

The Training of Chiliqui. London: George Philip and Son, 1929. Pp. 288.

The Verdict of the Sea. London: Hurst and Blackett, 1927. Pp. 288.

Three Came to Ville Marie. Toronto: Oxford University Press, 1941. Pp. 391.

What Fools Men Are. By Sinclair Murray (pseud.). London: Sampson Low, 1933. Pp. 316. Film script with same title by Sinclair Murray (pseud.), 1935.

Whispering Lodge. By Sinclair Murray (pseud.). Toronto: Ryerson, 1927. Pp. 336.

With Love From Rachel. By Sinclair Murray (pseud.). Toronto: Oxford University Press, 1938. Pp. 312.

Translated from the French

Felix-Antoine Savard. *Boss of the River*. Translated by Alan Sullivan. Toronto: Ryerson, 1947. Pp. 131.

Other Writings Cited in Text

"In the Matter of Alan Sullivan." *Ontario Library Review* 14 (November, 1929).

"John A. Pearson, Master Builder." *The Yearbook of Canadian Art*. Toronto: The Toronto Arts and Letters Club, 1913.

Notes written in an exercise book while Sullivan was in Monte Carlo. 1947. A copy is in the author's files.

The Law and the Prophet. Unpublished religious drama. 1944.

"To My Children—A Parental Whimsy." Unpublished poem. 1941. A copy is in the author's files.

Typescript of an address (ca. 1935) to a women's organization, "The League," presided over by Mrs. Dawson Scott. A copy is in the author's files.

Works by Others

Allen, Walter. *Reading a Novel*. London: Phoenix House, 1963.

A.J.J. Review of Alan Sullivan, *The Fur Masters*. In *The Irish Press*, Dublin. May 24, 1938.

Anon. Review of Alan Sullivan, *Three Came to Ville Marie*. In *The Sign*, Union City, New Jersey. February 19, 1943.

Anon. Review of Alan Sullivan, *The Fur Masters*. In *Inverness Courier*, Inverness, Scotland. May 10, 1938.

Anon. "The Great Barrier." Review of the film *The Great Barrier*. In Canada's Weekly London, England. February 12, 1937.

Bliss, Michael. Introduction to Alan Sullivan, *The Rapids*. Toronto: University of Toronto Press, 1972.

Caswell, Edward. *Canadian Singers and Their Songs*. Toronto: McClelland and Stewart, 1925.

C.W.G. "Rialto Feature Canadian Epic." Review of the film *The Great Barrier*. In *The Edmonton Journal*, April 4, 1937.

Eldon, Donald. "The Career of Francis H. Clergue." *Explorations and Entrepreneurial History* 3 (April, 1951).

Grove, Frederick Philip. *In Search of Myself*. Toronto: Macmillan, 1946.

————— . *It Needs To Be Said*. Toronto: Macmillan, 1929.

————— . Unpublished Lecture. University of Manitoba Library, Grove Collection, Box 22.

Hill, Douglas. "Gritted Teeth on the Pig Farm." Review of Aritha Van Herk, *Judith*. In *Saturday Night* 3 (November 1978).

H.O.H. "Barbering and Gold Rush." Review of Alan Sullivan, *Cariboo Road*. In *The Montreal Daily Star*, July 13, 1946.

Liddell Hart, Lady Kathleen. Notes entitled "Some Memories of my father, Alan Sullivan." 1976. A copy is in the author's files.

Klinck, Carl F. *Literary History of Canada*. Toronto: University of Toronto Press, 1965.

Munro, Janet. "Building the C.P.R." Review of Alan Sullivan, *The Great Divide*. In *Saturday Night* 50 (October 19, 1935).

Nye, Russell B. *Notes on a Rationale for a Popular Culture*. Bowling Green, Ohio: Popular Culture Association, 1970.

Pratt, E. J. *Towards the Last Spike*. Toronto: Macmillan, 1952.

Stevenson, John. A. "Alan Sullivan, Poet, Engineer." *Saturday Night* 62 (August 23, 1947).

Sullivan, Barry. Address at Cremation Service of Bessie Sullivan, March 20, 1974. A copy is in the author's files.

————— . *And Then We Went*. Privately printed, 1925. A copy is in the author's files.

————— . Notes written during the summer of 1947 in Monte Carlo. A copy is in the author's files.

Sullivan, Barry, and R. J. Sells. Transcript of a taped conversation between Barry Sullivan and R. J. Sells, 1947. A copy is in the author's files.

Wilson, Ethel. "A Cat Among the Falcons." In A. J. M. Smith (ed.), *Masks of Fiction*. Toronto: McClelland and Stewart, 1961.

Index